BEING NAKED

A nine week journey towards self-awareness

Janis Altman

W9-CBH-912

"It is never too late to be
what you might have been."

GEORGE ELIOT

AMP&RSAND, INC.

Chicago, Illinois

ISBN 978-0-9761235-9-0

Book Design: David Robson, Robson Design
Book Cover Design and Illustrations: Dalia Sabari

Published by
Ampersand, Inc.
1050 North State Street, Chicago IL 60610
Suzanne T. Isaacs, Publisher
www.ampersandworks.com

Published in the United States of America

DEDICATION

To my sons, Adam and Josh,
and to "HUSBAND"

ACKNOWLEDGMENTS

First and foremost, I thank Hashem who has given me my yesterdays, today and tomorrows.

Thank you to my b'shert, my love, my husband, Eli Katz, whose support and encouragement are constant, even at three in the morning.

I am forever grateful to my mother, Elissa Yellin, who continues to inspire me and serve as a role model.

To my son, Adam Altman, whose compassion and generosity of spirit are a continuous source of inspiration; to Jamie, my daughter-in-law, who has built a beautiful family; to my two delicious grandchildren, Finley and Shai, who bring light and joy into my life; and to Josh Altman, my spiritual, kind, loving son, who instills in me the desire to be a better human being. To these precious children and grandchildren I offer thanks for giving me the blessings of nachas and pride and for teaching me about our limitless capacity for love.

Thank you Ilan Pekker, whose wisdom and intelligence and insight have been a great gift to me.

Heidi Rosenberg, MD, FACOG, a doctor who spends every single day bringing babies into this world and raising two great sons of her own, thank you for always being a friend who is present, honest and honorable.

Thank you Linda, my Challah Mamma and soul sister, and to her wonderful family.

Thank you Rose, my life-long friend, honest and wise woman, who has given me great editorial advice in living and in writing.

Thank you, especially, to all my close friends who have earned my respect and love for their integrity, wisdom and ability to listen with care and kindness.

Thank you Dalia Sabari, an extraordinary, creative illustrator and designer who "gets it." She is the epitome of style and grace.

Thank you Ben Katz who is fast as heck on the computer and knows everything about grammar.

Thank you Suzie Isaacs for turning my manuscript into a book and David Robson for your elegant design.

To Linda Mensch, who is her name and so much more, thank you for believing in all my projects.

And finally and mostly, my gratitude and respect to all my clients who had the courage and desire to grow and to change and share their journey with me.

TABLE OF CONTENTS

He finds a comrade.
Now he beats the drum, now he stops.
Now he sobs, now he sings.
I CHING: 64. CHUNG FU/INNER TRUTH

PREFACE

Hi and welcome to *Being Naked.* My name is Janis Altman, and I wrote this book for people who want a process for making healthy changes in their lives.

This book will support your efforts to develop a deeper and clearer understanding of who you are.

When I first considered writing a book, I had no intention of writing this particular one. In fact, I had planned to write something entirely different – a book of stories, real-life stories, bringing to the page the multitude of voices I have had the privilege of encountering in my years of counseling.

But books, like life, rarely unfurl in the straight lines we sometimes wish they would. Instead, they are born and then often are driven more by necessity than intent.

What has emerged is not just those individual stories of healing, but a more important, perhaps necessary work, showing the *path* from which healing begins.

Being part of the process of my clients' growth has always felt a bit like magic to me. Of course, looking back, there was no magic at all. It was simply faith in their healing, their achievements, and their ability to think and experience life beyond their immediate circumstances.

Believing in others, even when they could not believe in themselves, brought me to understand the wonder of risk. In my world, risk is not bungee jumping or parachuting or driving racecars, for that matter. It's about exposing what exists within, about opening up space where creative energy is stored in both body and mind.

The lessons I've learned in over 25 years of practice have coincided, not so surprisingly, with the trials and triumphs of my clients.

Movement

I'll never forget my experience as the director of dance-movement therapy at a sleep-away camp for emotionally disturbed children. I had just finished graduate school and was very interested in how movement could be used as a tool for communication, a new idea at that time.

The children in my charge ranged from those with neurobiological disturbances to those who'd been ravaged by the effects of abuse. There were also children who were labeled emotionally disturbed.

There was one boy, David, whose physical demeanor was that of an adorable seven-year-old, but his movements were punctuated by robot-like gestures. He sounded like E.T. He dressed in layers and layers of clothes. He wore his pajamas, two shirts, a sweater, and was hesitant to take off his jacket when he came in from outside. I had a terrible tug inside me telling me this little boy had so much to say, so much to be.

Because of his bizarre behavior, David had been labeled as emotionally disturbed. Disturbed by what? That's what I wanted to know.

I thought if David could open up his range of movement, then maybe he could open up emotionally. I had an album by Babatunde Olatunji, an amazing Nigerian percussionist. Everyday I led a group of seven children in a dance/movement therapy session. I played music and had the children follow my lead. The essence of the exercise was to create a safe atmosphere where these children would feel free to move and express themselves. As their movement repertoire grew, their ability to express themselves would also grow.

David was in this group. When I played the Olatunji album, David responded by swinging his arms in rhythm with Olatunji's beat. After a few days, David's sweater got in the way of his new movement so he peeled off the sweater. Now he could really swing his arms. The broader range of movement was a new experience for him. A few weeks later, as I made the music louder, I encouraged David to make a sound with his voice while he was doing a movement. I wanted David's entire self to be involved in his movement – his mind, his body, his spirit. After a few weeks, David started beating the mat that I had placed on the floor beneath him. One afternoon, he started crying and said, "This is the way my daddy hits my mommy." His arms were moving in full swing. As the layers of clothes were removed, David's secret came out, and the long road to healing began.

David's clothes had become part of his mask, hiding a secret that, once revealed, could only free him from its burden. But what was it about the tangible nature of David's clothes, taking them off piece-by-piece, that empowered him so?

David's story reaffirms what I've observed in my years of private practice: the physical act of doing, and not just talking and thinking and wondering, is a truly effective way for people to reach their goal, whether the goal is working through relationships, moving on in careers, or even overcoming severe emotional issues.

Though I am still in love with the wonder of my clients' stories, I feel the same tug inside me as I felt at Camp Rainbow. I feel as though *everyone* should have the same opportunity to grow and move forward in their lives, to have the tools to reclaim a part of the self, to create one's own story.

Growth and Change

Over the years, I learned that directed homework, sometimes journal assignments, gave my clients a necessary structure from which they could find their own creative force, with their own capacity to solve problems, and move ahead.

This is how *Being Naked* was born. From there, I had to ask myself: what is the central theme to this kind of journey, these types of exercises, and movement sessions? More importantly, what have all my clients held in common? Simply, these exercises are guided steps through transitions, whether you are forced into that transition from catastrophe and hardship (many people came to me after September 11th) or have simply warmed to the idea of change.

In my excitement of deciding what to include in this book and others, I keep myself up at night. A flood of experiences wash over me before I drift into sleep. Although this book is practical in nature, what drives the journal assignments are stories that my clients found locked inside, wrapped in sweaters both metaphorical and real, and too often cloaked by time.

The Role of Therapy

Because I am a therapist, it's fair to ask, "What is therapy?" There are many ways to answer this question, but here's one that I think will be useful as you work through the exercises in this book: *Therapy is a process for reclaiming control of your life, for assuming more responsibility for your actions and for making better choices.*

Most people turn to therapy when they realize they have become stuck. They want to move forward but keep finding obstacles in their path.

How do you know when you've gotten stuck? When you can't make a commitment to a partner, when you can't choose a career after graduating from college, when you can't stand your job, when conversations with your best friend always make you feel miserable, when you feel a deep sense of sadness for "no apparent reason," when you gravitate towards a relationship that is toxic, when you know in your heart that what you really want is to be is a stand-up comic but you just don't have the courage to tell your spouse or parent. These are the kinds of issues that bedevil us. It's our lot. But it doesn't mean that we have to put up with being stuck or unhappy.

Therapy was invented to overcome the challenges we create for ourselves. In therapy, we explore our inner thoughts and feelings and try to bring them to the surface where we can talk about them.

I am not a believer in spending an endless amount of time and money on digging through one's childhood woes, but I am a believer in mining those aspects of mind, body and spirit to find a true self, a naked self, if you will. It is from this place that we emerge as only we can imagine ourselves to be. Each of us is unique and armed with the power of possibility.

Janis Altman
Englewood, NJ
August 2008

HOW TO USE THIS BOOK

This Book Is for You

Being Naked is designed for the brave individual who feels ready for an experience that is new, exciting and positive. It can help you if you are going through any kind of transition, getting over a break up, or recovering from an illness. It will support your efforts to develop a deeper and clearer understanding of who you are.

Being Naked is divided into five main chapters and is structured as a nine week course. With the exception of Chapter 5, each chapter opens with a brief discussion of the topic followed by JOURNALING IN PRACTICE, which is a true-to-life example of how journal exercises can be used effectively. This is followed by exercises, most often questions, although some require visualization and similar work.

You are in charge of this process, so discipline in working through the sections falls on your shoulders alone. Sometimes when you think you are finished with a section, you uncover something you need to learn. When this happens, don't stop. Push yourself further.

The structure of *Being Naked* forces you to direct your thinking, in fact discipline your thinking, as you reflect on the changes happening in your life. What makes this book unique is that it is yours.

What You Can Achieve

My hope is that by reading this book and completing the exercises, you will become a healthier, happier person. You will understand yourself with greater clarity. You will be in a better position to make wise choices, embrace new challenges and avoid behaviors that might prove harmful.

It will help you remember the skills that you already have within yourself. By crystallizing and articulating your thoughts, you will be able to express what is on your mind more clearly and forcefully, increasing your sense of self-awareness.

Guideposts

Here are some truisms that you may find useful as you begin
your journey.

1. Sometimes bad things really do happen to good people.
   Don't let it stop you from being the best that you can be.

2. You cannot make anyone love you.

3. When you do find love, love with all your heart and soul.

4. Don't be afraid to feel vulnerable. It's the key to allowing love
   to happen.

5. Sometimes you have to be with someone through all the
   seasons before you can say "I love you."

6. Evil does exist, but it doesn't mean you have to make it your
   dating partner.

7. Progress is good, as long as it doesn't get in the way of your life.

8. Just when you feel that you can't hold on anymore, remember
   that the sun is just around the corner, waiting to shine its
   glorious rays on you.

9. Be careful what you say – the Universe is listening.

10. Your body remembers what your mind chooses to forget.

11. Only you can bring meaning to your life.

12. There are always consequences to lies.

13. Be open to the suffering of others. Have compassion, even if
    you can't relieve someone else's suffering.

14. Be responsible for everything you do, but realize that you are
    not responsible for others' mistakes.

15. Be prepared. Do your homework – in school, at work,
    and above all, in life.

"Learn to get in touch with the silence within yourself and know that everything in this life has a purpose."
ELIZABETH KUBLER-ROSS

GETTING STARTED

Your Journey

Your story is bound to have a fascinating main character, a dynamic plot and a rich, resounding voice. It will emerge as you progress through your own personal journey with opportunities to express your feelings, thoughts, hopes and dreams with imagination and creativity.

Perhaps you have kept journals before, recording your thoughts and feelings, wishes and desires. It may have been a travel journal where you wrote down all the sights and sounds of a new place, or an online journal, where you shared your thoughts with others in the never land of cyberspace. But this one will be different.

Our life transitions are opportunities for taking stock of ourselves, assessing how the past came to be; and redirecting what lies ahead. *Being Naked* guides you through the process, giving you room to grow but challenging you to address the obstacles in your way. Writing helps you to clean house by taking inventory of the contents of your mind, deciding what to keep and what to toss so you can open up precious space.

This is a chance to discover your true self, manifest a new wisdom and nourish your dreams.

The Benefits of Writing

It is no accident that ancient cultures throughout the world have revered the written word, assigning it cosmic authority and mystical strength. The written word embodies power, energy and influence.

Whether it's carved in stone, written in ink or typed on a personal computer, the written word is undeniably and uniquely powerful.

In telling your story, you will take the positive, inexhaustible energy of the written word and put it work for you in a healthy, constructive way.

If the written word was good enough for William Shakespeare, Jane Austen, Virginia Wolf, Eudora Welty and J.D. Salinger, it should be good enough for us. Why did God instruct Moses to inscribe the Ten Commandments onto two stone tablets? Because when something is written down, it automatically becomes more powerful, more useful and immediately beneficial.

What Writing Can Do for You

1. *Writing is a form of therapy* – in the sense that it can help you become more conscious, more aware and more focused. Writing definitely qualifies as a form of therapy. As Anne Frank wrote, "I want to write, but more than that, I want to bring out all kinds of things that lie buried deep in my heart."

2. *Writing is a form of meditation* – because it helps clear your mind, quiet your thoughts and achieve greater clarity. Writing is without doubt a form of meditation. Although we tend to imagine professional writers as obsessive wretches working against impossible deadlines, most of the writers I know are gentle, relaxed people who seem generally oblivious to the pressures of life around them. Since the act of writing requires them to distinguish constantly between what is important and what is unimportant, writers develop an instinct for staying focused on what really matters.

3. *Writing creates a tangible record of your progress* – because it is concrete proof of the work you are doing to become happier, healthier and more self-aware. Every thought or stream of thoughts that you capture in writing is incontrovertible evidence of your effort.

Your Gift to Yourself

When you glance through this book you will notice that after each writing exercise there is a short space for making notes. The space is there so you can elaborate on your thoughts without having to look for more paper. However, if you are uncomfortable jotting down your thoughts here, use a companion notebook.

You can also decorate your book. Add photos, drawings, maps, stickers, collage or anything you like! Your writing is your gift to yourself – so feel free to follow your instincts and be creative.

A True Story

I believe so much in the power of writing that it is an essential part of my practice. This story is an example of how writing puts us in touch with our natural self – the real person hidden under the defense mechanisms we invent for coping with our lives.

Elizabeth came to me when her boyfriend left her. She was 32. For the past 10 years she had lived with her boyfriend. Her life revolved around attending to his needs. She had worked part-time as a waitress, but the money she earned was not enough to support herself.

For Elizabeth, the breakup was devastating. When she first arrived in my office, she was severely depressed. She had stopped eating. She was unable to work. She could barely articulate her loss.

During our first session, I asked Elizabeth to make a list of goals so she could begin the process of transitioning out of this difficult time. But she was too despondent to focus on the task of making a list.

Then I asked her to think of one short-term goal, no more. I told her to write it on a piece of paper. The goal she wrote down was to continue therapy.

By the next week, she had accomplished her first goal. Now she was ready to expand her list. She wrote that she would get back on a healthy diet and start an exercise program. Soon she had restored physical health and sense of well-being to the point where she could add more goals to her written list. In short order she rewrote her resume and began looking for a full-time job.

Fulfilling each goal on the list gave her the energy, motivation and confidence she needed to continue the process.

When she was at last restored enough to ponder a new life beyond the one she had been living, I asked Elizabeth to describe her ideal future. She wrote that in a dream, she had seen herself leading a child-centered company.

Through her writing exercises, she amplified and added detail to her dream. Over time, she prepared herself to make the dream come true by taking a series of concrete steps that landed her a job at a major entertainment company, where she works on projects for young audiences. She has since been promoted to several leadership positions in that company.

The writing exercises kept Elizabeth firmly on track throughout the long and difficult process of reclaiming her life. Eventually, she was able to transform the vision in her dream into tangible reality. It was a long process, but she was able to achieve her deepest desires.

A Commitment You Can Keep

Unlike promising to go to the gym five times a week, writing is a commitment that you can keep more easily. In a recent edition of The Writer's Almanac, Garrison Keillor shared this little story with his readers:

Graham Greene realized early in his writing career that if he wrote just 500 words a day, he would have written several million words in just a few decades. So he developed a routine of writing for exactly two hours every day, and he was so strict about stopping after exactly two hours that he often stopped writing in the middle of a sentence. And at that pace, he managed to publish 26 novels, as well as numerous short stories, plays, screenplays, memoirs, and travel books.

Now let's begin.

"He who knows others is wise.
He who knows himself is enlightened."
LAO TZU, *Tao Te Ching*

CHAPTER 1

Before you begin, think about where you are. Are you comfortable? Is it quiet? Be sure you feel at ease. In silence, thoughts flow more gracefully. Let your thoughts pour onto the page before you. Try not to analyze what you're writing. Forget about grammar or spelling. Just keep your stream of consciousness flowing.

Express yourself as fully and freely as you can. Don't cross out words, thoughts or ideas. Your first choice of expression is usually right. Don't be harsh with yourself by critiquing your thought process or writing style.

When you think you are done, push yourself to go a little further. Sometimes when you think you have completed a thought, you are just at the beginning. If it gets a little scary, that's good because it means you are touching something real. Go beyond to the place that resonates for you.

Have fun, relax, and enjoy your journey!

Skimming the Surface

Is the person looking back from the mirror the same person others see at work, school, or walking down the street? What about your clothes, the way you hold your body, your smile – are these artifacts of your past, your present, or how you imagine yourself in the future?

Is there a difference between what you and others see outside and what lies within? The answer to all of these questions is likely a resounding YES!

Having an "outside" self and an "inside" self is not so uncommon. In fact, most of us do. Very often, the "inside" self holds the wisdom and creativity that the "outside" self needs in order to flourish.

And yet it is this "inside" self that we most often neglect. In our busy lives – working, studying, raising families, balancing family with career, and socializing – it is no wonder that many of us neglect seeing beyond the mirror image, beyond our immediate self-perceptions, or beyond the perceptions that are reflected back from others.

The business of everyday life does not offer much help when you want to look beyond the superficial and harvest your inner resources. That is why getting reacquainted with yourself, both inside and out, is critical in times of transition.

Before we can make use of the wisdom that is inside us, we must first find a starting point.

This chapter will give you the opportunity to explore aspects of yourself that you may have taken for granted, or those that were simply too obvious to see clearly. In Week One, you will take stock of yourself through your own eyes and the eyes of those close to you.

Each exercise is broken into three to six sections that are designed to be used over the course of a week. Do them daily, if possible, but make it work within your schedule. You may speed up the process or slow it down by spending more time on sections that resonate with a specific change happening in your life now.

WEEK ONE

AN EXPLORATION OF SELF: *WHO AM I?*

This is the mother of all questions. Since the beginning of time, great thinkers have sought to answer this profound question. But as they have found (and you will, too) the answer lies within.

When someone asks us who we are, it is likely that we initially think in terms of our identity. "Identity" is a word loaded with meaning and possibility. It is both concept and evidence. Our identity is laminated onto our driver's license; it is embossed on our birth certificate. It is on our work or school I.D. card, insurance card, passport, email account, Face Book image, and YouTube. It is the "evidence" of who we are.

We are not the sum of our height, weight, hair color and address! Yet those identifying markers are part of what shape us. For instance, my last name identifies my family. My height is predetermined by genetics. But what if I am particularly tall, do I "identify" as a "tall person?"

What does my address say about me? Do I live on Park Avenue in New York City? Or on Main Street in Boise? All of these "identifying" markers not only convey to others who we are, or where we are from, but they also reinforce what we, ourselves, may have always believed to be "true."

But be careful. We may need to reexamine what is "true" – that is, our identity and the roles we may have accepted without even realizing it. Indeed, each of us is a daughter or a son. Many of us are also wives or husbands, mothers or fathers, brothers or sisters. But what pieces of our identity have we passively accepted? What roles do we play just because these pieces were handed to us? What aspects of our identity have we not even considered because they are too familiar, too near?

Think of yourself as an empty house. Pretend that messages people gave you when you were a child are "furniture" they moved into your house when the house was new. Eventually, who you are is made up of an accumulation of these messages, words and images that other people have placed in your home over the years. There are even some messages you have brought in yourself, some of them positive and some negative.

Nevertheless, some messages have nothing to do with reality and some don't allow you to feel good about yourself. But they are still in your home. Remember, you are the gatekeeper of your home. You can choose to keep what you want and throw away the pieces that cause too much clutter.

You can choose which messages go and which ones stay. With self-awareness comes power. You must learn to harness that power in order to start shaping, or reshaping as the case may be, your identity.

This chapter is about house cleaning. The choices you make about what furniture to keep will reflect who you are and who you are becoming.

> "Action may not always bring happiness;
> but there is no happiness without action."
> BENJAMIN DISRAELI

JOURNALING IN PRACTICE

When Joel first came to me, he made it clear that he was not interested in what I had to say and he was there only at the behest of his wife. Joel seemed like a difficult case to manage with only questions and talking, since he was not a particularly verbal person. Amidst the awkward silence, I handed him a blank sheet of paper and a pen and asked him to draw a picture of his mother. In two seconds flat, Joel rendered a neat circle with two dots for eyes and a mouth almost as big as the first circle. I smiled and said, "So she was a big mouth, huh?" Joel's crossed brow broadened into a smile. We could finally begin to uncover what was beneath Joel's tough exterior.

Pen and paper gave Joel a physical space to respond, illustrating his own life in pictures and words. As a self-proclaimed "skeptic," Joel needed to make the connection quickly between his "homework" and therapy.

Within a few sessions of using journal exercises, we began to uncover the problems in his relationship. Joel's mother had been very controlling and though he resented it, he continued to be drawn to controlling women.

Joel used the exercises that follow to explore both his good and not so pleasant personality traits. This later helped him see not only how he kept repeating relationship patterns, but also what resources he could use to make changes.

Writing about his good qualities early in his journal therapy gave him positive resources to work with when things got a little tougher down the road.

"Nothing has a stronger influence psychologically on
their environment and especially on their children than
the unlived life of the parent."
CARL JUNG

QUESTIONS & EXERCISES I

As children, our teachers, parents and friends had expectations for
us to live up to. Maybe you fulfilled those expectations. Or maybe
you rebelled against those expectations, deciding to reject all advice
regardless of outcome.

Either way, it is impossible to escape the influence of those around us,
especially when we are young. The people who surround us have an
impact on the person we become; their expectations, whether heeded
or not, contribute to building or destroying our self-esteem.

What we want to accomplish in this first exercise is to open the window,
to have a glimpse of the real you, the person inside, the child-like
dreamer. This is the "you" *before* the expectations of others became
your expectations, too. This is not to say that all expectations of others
should be shunned, since all of us have them.

The following questions will allow you to have a look at yourself without
those expectations.

EXPLORING YOUR SELF

There was once a Cherokee grandfather speaking with his grandson. He said, "Listen, child, for what I speak is truth. There are two wolves in you. The first wolf wears deceit, cruelty, fear and anger, while the second one wears truth, kindness, bravery and patience. And they're fighting inside of you."

"But grandfather, who wins?"

"Simply, my child, the answer lies in which one you feed."

Who are you? For example, I am an unmarried 30-year-old woman. I am a 35-year-old successful banker or broker or artist. I am a 23-year-old student. I am a mother of three children. I am a 50-year-old divorced mother of five.

Who are you?

I am _____

_____

_____

_____

_____

Are you happy with the way your life is playing out? Yes? No? **Why?**

_____

_____

_____

_____

_____

Do you believe you can change your destiny? Yes? **How?** No? **Why?**
Write down how you might make a change.

_____

_____

_____

_____

_____

Are you living out the dreams and the aspirations of your mother or father? For example, as you were growing up did your mother or father want you to be a doctor, a lawyer, a real estate agent, an artist, a musician? Or did your father not care what you became? Was he absent? Was your mother absent? **Write down what they wanted you to become.**

_____

_____

_____

_____

Describe what you are doing now.

_____

_____

_____

_____

Describe how your parents' aspirations affected your life. Are you doing what your parents wanted or what you wanted for yourself?

_____

_____

_____

_____

_____

List five personality traits that you like about yourself.
For example: compassionate, funny, driven.

_____

_____

_____

_____

_____

List five traits you _don't_ like about yourself.
For example: anger, bitterness, shut down.

_____

_____

_____

_____

_____

Choose two of the traits that you don't like about yourself. How have these two out of five personality characteristics you don't like affected your life? For example: Cannot make a commitment in a relationship; have never been in a long-term relationship.

_____

_____

_____

_____

_____

You can either stop here and think about these important answers or go to the next section.

NOTES

QUESTIONS & EXERCISES II

THE VOICES OF OTHERS

Other people often try to tell us who we are. Sometimes, these messages become self-fulfilling prophecies. This can be positive or negative, depending, of course, on the messages we receive and whether or not we believe them.

Who in your life compliments you? Write the names of people in your world who say kind things to you. For example: My best friend, Rose, lets me know what a devoted friend I am. List the compliments. Don't be shy.

_____

_____

_____

_____

_____

Did you compliment anyone today? This week? This month? Write what you said and to whom you said it.

_____

_____

_____

_____

_____

Who criticizes you? List them by name.

_____

_____

_____

_____

_____

Do you believe their criticisms? Why?

_____

_____

_____

_____

_____

Can you shut off all the voices that criticize you? Yes? No?
**If yes, list how you will accomplish this. If no, list why it is so
difficult for you.**

_____

_____

_____

_____

Have you criticized anyone today? This week? This month?
Write down what you said and to whom.

_____

_____

_____

_____

_____

NOTES

QUESTIONS & EXERCISES III

THE HERE AND NOW

Where we are today may be different from where we were yesterday. Each moment brings its own state of mind and its own frame of reality. We may react completely differently today to the same news we heard yesterday because we feel differently today than we did then.

We are forever evolving, shifting, moving. The human spirit is composed of flowing energy, which makes us fluid beings.

How do you describe where you are at present? For example: Is this a happy time in your life? Do you like who your friends are? Are there things you want to do that you're not doing?

_____

_____

_____

_____

_____

Who in your life brings you the most joy?
What are their names? List them.

_____

_____

_____

_____

_____

What about your life do you like best? What don't you like?

_____

_____

_____

_____

_____

Can you change the things you don't like? What would it take for you to change them? For example: I don't like where I live. I have some friends who treat me cruelly.

_____

_____

_____

_____

_____

What are the first three things you need to do in order to have the life you truly want now? Remember that old adage, _"there's no time like the present."_

_____

_____

_____

_____

_____

What are your long-term goals? What are the first five things you need to do?

_____

_____

_____

_____

_____

NOTES

QUESTIONS & EXERCISES IV

WORK AND SCHOOL: THE IDENTITY PROBLEM

Are you *what you do?* Does your work life or school life define you? Do you delve into your job or identity at school so much that you become callous to deeper desires, real feelings? Teasing out your identity when surrounded by a familiar place or familiar people is not so easy. Although ties to work and community are often good things, it is important to know how you relate to them and how to examine more closely whether you are forging ahead or simply hiding.

If you have a job, do you love your work or is it a place where you escape your inner most thoughts? Suppose you were not working, what would you do with your day? Describe that day. Would it be like "Ferris Bueller's Day Off" or is there a huge pile of laundry waiting for you at home?

_____

_____

_____

_____

_____

If you are still in school or college, describe what you want to do after you have graduated.

_____

_____

_____

_____

_____

NOTES

QUESTIONS & EXERCISES V

RELATIONSHIPS

A relationship is defined by an emotional state or feeling toward a prominent person in our lives. Relationships are important, because as human beings, we are social creatures. The bonds we make with others are what make life worthwhile.

When these relationships demand excessive compromise, they can obscure the relationship we have with ourselves. Some people demand so much of us that there is just not enough of our "self" to go around.

This is not always easy to see, particularly if these demanding people are very familiar to you, if they are close friends or family.

Are you compromising your identity for a relationship? How does it feel? For example: have you stopped seeing your friends because of one particular person?

_____

_____

_____

_____

_____

How often do you _not_ say what you feel and instead say what others want to hear? When does that happen?

_____

_____

_____

_____

_____

What relationship makes you feel disconnected from yourself?
For example: Whenever I am with my girlfriend, we always do
whatever she wants me to do.

_____

_____

_____

_____

_____

**Who are those people who make you feel disconnected?
List them.**

_____

_____

_____

_____

_____

Who in your life manipulates you? Manipulation means
"to influence or manage shrewdly or deviously."

_____

_____

_____

_____

_____

Why do you still spend time with them?

_____

_____

_____

_____

_____

What do you gain from these relationships?

_____

_____

_____

_____

_____

NOTES

WEEK TWO

Self-Esteem: *What Is It?*

Every person has an opinion of him or herself. Self-esteem is how you view yourself. Healthy, positive self-esteem allows you to take pride in the person you are. It empowers you to accept responsibility for your actions, take risks, seek challenges and be in full command of your life. With a healthy sense of self-esteem, you know you can trust your inner wisdom to guide you in all your decisions and opinions.

Some of us are fortunate and have plenty of self-esteem. We take charge of our lives, forge ahead with confidence, and are ready for the next challenge life brings. For some of us, building self-esteem is a process and one that requires assessment and redirection at different points in time.

Even people with high self-esteem may find that during life transitions, the ground underfoot can get a bit shaky. Life is not always easy and can dish out its share of hardship and tragedy. No matter what point on the self-esteem continuum you find yourself, having the tools to build – or to rebuild – the foundations of a strong self are necessary.

Low Self-Esteem: *Where Did It Come From?*

There are times when we give other people too much power by allowing their words to diminish our self-worth. Words only have as much power as we give them. The words we believe can shape our self-esteem for the better or for the worse. If we hold negative words to be true, the words will take on undeserved meaning and will inevitably result in low self-esteem.

So, where does low self-esteem come from? As we grow up, our teachers, parents and friends have expectations of us. Their expectations can have an impact on what we believe, who we become and how we live our lives. Sometimes we are expected to be someone we are not – someone we cannot be nor have any desire to become. Conflict arises when we try to be true to ourselves and at the same time please others. Inevitably, we will find a disappointed friend, an angry parent, an uncomplimentary teacher, or worse still, an unfulfilled self.

Expectations from others may have either a positive or a negative impact. They send us messages that hold either positive or negative content. The impact of negative messages may leave us feeling defeated, misguided or unsure of ourselves.

A negative message does not have to be literal, written, or spoken in order for it to penetrate. We are innately conscious of the relationship between a person's behavior and feelings. On the other hand, behavior and attitudes can be misunderstood. What if our interpretation is wrong?

One child whose mother is not home after school may interpret the message as: "My Mom chooses not to be with me. I am of no value." And yet another might think it's because, "My mom trusts me to take care of myself and that means I'm smart and reliable."

This example shows why it's important to examine the message *and your response to the message*. A more independent personality (child or adult) may embrace being left alone, as in the example above. Some of us, however, may feel more comfortable when someone else is there to provide support, comfort or guidance.

It is important to know how our responses and perceptions play into the process of building confidence. This is why getting to know yourself is intertwined with building self-esteem.

Building Self-Esteem

Consider this – you *are* what you believe. No one – other than yourself – can truly enhance or diminish your self-esteem unless you choose to let him or her. This may be difficult to implement at times. If you struggle with your self-esteem, the process of building self-esteem will require practice. The time you invest in believing the positive messages that you will be sending yourself will be rewarded a hundred fold.

In order to have positive self-esteem, choose only to believe positive thoughts – words that encourage, enhance and support you. Listen to the voices within you and try to determine the "quality" of the message being sent. For instance, you make a mistake at work or on a homework assignment and you catch yourself before handing it in. In that single moment, a number of different messages may be sent. Listen to that message. Does the voice say, "I'm so stupid. What do I think I'm doing?" or does the voice say, "Good save. Glad I caught that in time"?

In this example, the same mistake was made, the same error caught, but the response of the inner voice was entirely different.

Think about the effect of the voice of praise for catching the mistake. Isn't it easier to move to the next task with confidence with that tiny note of praise rather than a punitive one?

Our innermost life is filled with thoughts and voices, sometimes jumbled, other times straightforward. These voices may give us positive or negative messages. In this section, the goal is to identify negative messages and reshape them into positive forces that will propel you forward.

Sometimes, it may be necessary simply to shut out the negative voices. This is true for not only our own, inner voices, but also for voices from the outside world. All too often, it is the negative messages from other people that are internalized and then reinforced by our own inner voice.

Constructive criticism can be helpful, but criticism meant to undermine our self-esteem can have toxic effects. Tune in to the messages sent by your peers, supervisors, teachers, parents and friends. Are they sending you positive messages, giving useful criticism that is meant to foster your growth?

Or are they sending messages that hinder your growth? Once you tune in to where the positive and negative messages are coming from, you can begin to develop a strategy to increase the positive and reject the negative messages.

It may not be possible to quit your job or leave school because your supervisor or teacher is sending negative messages, but you CAN avoid internalizing those messages. Just because someone with authority over you (supervisor, teacher, parent) attempts to send negative messages, make it your mission not to accept them. It is *their* problem, not yours.

Don't let their voices become yours. You have the power to create your own positive inner voice.

Positive Reinforcement Exercises

One tool for building self-esteem is to tune out and/or reject negative messages. An even better tool is positive reinforcement.

Research supports how positive reinforcement works – repetition of positive statements generates familiarity. Once you become familiar with the sounds, the rhythms and, of course, the *effects* of positive language, your brain and "self" become much more willing and able to accept it.

This is important to remember, particularly if you are not accustomed to receiving positive messages. In fact, if you are in a place in your life where you bristle at hearing positive language directed at you, it will initially feel unwieldy. This will change very quickly. Positive reinforcement exercises are used widely, from corporate management training to elementary education. They are simple to do and they work!

Positive reinforcement sounds like this: "I like myself, I am smart, I am in control, I *can* do this job." It is *not*: "I *think* I will be in control, I *think* I can handle this."

Affirmations are phrases that are positive messages of strength. They are active words that command your spirit to believe. Use positive affirmations in all situations in your life – before a meeting, before a date, before and during any time you may feel yourself weakening.

Imagine you are going to a job interview. As you walk up the steps, you begin to feel anxious. Your palms are sweaty, your heart seems to be working a little harder, your thoughts race. Take a breath and tell yourself that you will be successful. If you repeat it like a mantra, over and over as you walk up the steps, you will tune out the self-doubting comments that needle their way into your mind. A positive affirmation is a powerful tool with dramatic results.

Have you ever watched an Olympic athlete in the minutes before an event? You will very often see the skater, the long-distance runner or the gymnast with head bowed, eyes closed, or looking intently ahead, but at no one in particular. They seem to be in deep focus. What is going through their minds? Very often, they are rehearsing their program, run or routine, imagining themselves completing their goal with absolute precision. This is a form of positive reinforcement.

No doubt, some of these champions will tell themselves in words, "You *will* succeed." One thing is certain – they are not rehearsing FALLING DOWN and they are not letting their inner voice say, "You're not going to make it." They are instead giving themselves lots of last minute positive reinforcement. The same technique can be used in everyday situations.

People with good self-esteem have a lot in common. They possess the courage to take risks and stand up for their ideals. They find it easy to imagine things working out well for them and as a result, they are more likely to act independently and to assume responsibility.

Because high self-esteem is visible to the outside world, a person who believes in herself will project that attitude and is more likely to be successful in school, jobs, and personal relationships.

In the book (and subsequent movie) *How To Succeed in Business without Really Trying*, the lead character is the mail room clerk at a large company. Every morning while shaving, he looks in the mirror and belts out the song, "I believe in you." Can you guess what happens? Eventually he becomes the company's CEO. That's the power of positive self-esteem.

In a more current movie, *Legally Blonde*, Reese Witherspoon plays the role of Elle Woods. Elle has an epiphany that, because of her blonde hair, shapely body and Valley behavior, nobody has ever taken her seriously, not even her parents. She is determined to focus all her energy on her school work and become the most successful person she could be. Elle understands that her personal success is the best revenge. When she speaks at the closing ceremony at her graduation from Harvard, Elle says, "On our very first day at Harvard, a very wise professor quoted Aristotle: 'The law is reason, free from passion.' Well, no offense to Aristotle, but in my three years at Harvard I have come to find that passion is a key ingredient to the study and practice of law – and of life. It is with passion, courage of conviction, and a strong sense of self that we take our next step into the world, remembering that first impressions are not always correct. You must always have faith in people. And most importantly, you must always have faith in yourself."

JOURNALING IN PRACTICE

When Monica came to me, she was anxious, worried, and losing weight to the point where her health was compromised. After I sent her to an internist to rule out any organic problem, she returned to me even more befuddled, confused and not knowing why she was so unhappy.

In our early sessions, I asked Monica to describe herself. What she described was a "model" friend, coworker and wife – all of which she described through the eyes of her friends, coworkers and husband! Monica was a pleaser by all definitions. When finally describing herself from her own perspective, she said she felt like a patchwork quilt – a jumble of voices and opinions of which none were her own.

Monica was a very intelligent, attractive young woman and yet, she had no idea who Monica was. Her whole sense of self was tied to the opinions of others.

Monica's journal assignment included writing the positive and negative messages she remembered hearing when she was young (you will do this in the journal exercises that follow). When Monica arrived at our next session, she had a laundry list of messages critiquing her appearance, her school performance as a child, even her ideas! What we did with the exercise was to look at those messages and then to look at the reality of who she was. Her real childhood achievements as well as constant parental criticisms and demands to perform were disconnected from who she was.

Monica's response to the negative messages in her life was to be hyper-responsible, always vigilant, and "perfect." Although it may seem obvious in another person's life that the negative messages have damaging effects, it is often much more difficult to see in oneself. Monica was no exception. She knew the language of self-esteem and how negative and positive reinforcement can impact a person's confidence. Only by identifying specific messages directed at her and writing them down could she actually see the enormous disconnect between the words of expectations and criticisms and its tremendous impact.

"There are voices which we hear in solitude, but they grow faint and inaudible as we enter into the world."

RALPH WALDO EMERSON

As we move into the journal exercises, begin thinking about the messages you have heard throughout your lifetime. Which ones do you truly believe? If you were reinforced with good words, try to understand why. If you were shaped by negativity, think about ways to replace demoralizing thoughts with new, positive, self-affirming messages. The questions below will help you along the way.

QUESTIONS & EXERCISES I

Childhood

What messages did you hear as you were growing up? For instance, did you hear things like, "Be a good girl, be nice, respect your elders, don't fight with your brother"? These words are messages that formed our earliest thoughts and helped to shape our opinion of the person we are today.

Write three messages you remember hearing as a child and the names of the people who said them to you.

_____

_____

_____

_____

_____

Did these messages change when you got older? If so, how?

_____

_____

_____

_____

_____

List the names of teachers who supported you.

_____

_____

_____

_____

_____

**List the names of teachers who made you feel inadequate.
If someone said you were "bad," did you believe it?**
Examples: If your head weren't attached, you'd probably lose it.
Why can't you be as smart as your brother? Let the boys think they're
smarter than you are. Big boys don't cry. **If you believed messages
such as these, why?**

_____

_____

_____

_____

_____

List five negative messages you received while growing up.

_____

_____

_____

_____

_____

List five positive messages. Examples: You can do or be anything you want, all you need is to believe in yourself the way we believe in you.

_____

_____

_____

_____

_____

Did you believe these messages? What impact do these messages have on your life right now?

_____

_____

_____

_____

_____

NOTES

QUESTIONS & EXERCISES II

PARENTS

Your parents, or the persons who raised you, most likely had the biggest impact on your opinion of yourself. They gave you your first impressions of who you are.

What expectations did your parents have of you?

_____

_____

_____

_____

_____

Do you think you lived up to these expectations?
If so, how? If not, why?

_____

_____

_____

_____

_____

Did they cause you to feel inadequate? If so, in what way?

_____

_____

_____

_____

_____

Did their expectations have a positive effect on your achievements? How?

_____

_____

_____

_____

_____

NOTES

QUESTIONS & EXERCISES III

OFFICE/SCHOOL

Self-esteem in the workplace can make the difference between a promotion and getting fired. If you are a student, self-esteem can affect your grades and set the stage for your working life ahead. With positive self-esteem, you can believe in yourself enough to make courageous moves, to articulate your vision and help shape the social landscape or the direction of a company. You are as powerful as you believe you are.

If you have a manager/teacher, how does that person treat you?

_____

_____

_____

_____

_____

How does a pay raise make you feel about yourself? Is it as important as a positive review? Why or why not?

_____

_____

_____

_____

_____

Are you more comfortable at work or in a social situation? Why do you think this is the case?

_____

_____

_____

_____

_____

Does your self-esteem at work differ from that in social situations?

_____

_____

_____

_____

_____

What if you are not invited to an important meeting? How does that make you feel?

_____

_____

_____

_____

_____

Do people at work cause you to doubt yourself? Who?
What do they do to make you feel that way?

_____

_____

_____

_____

_____

What do you think you can do about it?

_____

_____

_____

_____

_____

NOTES

"It is easy – terribly easy – to shake a man's faith in himself.
To take advantage of that, to break a man's spirit, is devil's work."
GEORGE BERNARD SHAW

QUESTIONS & EXERCISES IV

FRIENDS

Friends and peer pressure can turn us into someone we don't recognize. These external factors can influence what we do and what we believe – for the positive or the negative. Friends are a strong force because we gravitate to them for one reason or another. Unlike family, we choose our friends for reasons that we are sometimes unaware.

Who are the people you most like to be around? Why?

_____

_____

_____

_____

_____

**Does anyone in your life continually put you down?
If so, who and in what way?**

_____

_____

_____

_____

_____

Do you believe their message? If so, why?

_____

_____

_____

_____

_____

Why do you keep these people in your life?

_____

_____

_____

_____

_____

What can you do to improve the situation?

_____

_____

_____

_____

_____

How do you feel when you believe you have disappointed someone? Do you think their expectations were fair?

_____

_____

_____

_____

_____

NOTES

QUESTIONS & EXERCISES V

IMAGINE...
**Find a photo of yourself
as a child. Paste it here.**

CHILD	RECENT

Look at yourself as a child. How have you changed?

_____

_____

_____

_____

_____

How have you stayed the same?

_____

_____

_____

_____

_____

What did you dream of becoming when you were at that age? As you look at this picture, do you remember any of the messages from people around you? What were those messages?

_____

_____

_____

_____

_____

Next to your childhood picture, paste a recent photo of yourself. What do you like about what you see? What don't you like?

_____

_____

_____

_____

_____

How can you change what you don't like? What is the first thing you need to do? Be realistic but go a step beyond where your instinct tells you to go.

_____

_____

_____

_____

_____

NOTES

QUESTIONS & EXERCISES VI

SELF-IMAGE

How you feel about yourself has a lot to do with how you see your physical self. Your facial expressions, body language, choice of clothing, smile and the way you walk are all reflections of your self-esteem. Though you may not be aware of how you feel about yourself, the expression of your self-esteem is visible to those around you.

Stand in front of a full-length mirror at home or perhaps in your gym. Look at yourself and think about what you see. What do you like about what you see?

_____

_____

_____

_____

_____

What don't you like?

_____

_____

_____

_____

_____

What would it take for you to feel comfortable in your body?

_____

_____

_____

_____

_____

**What do you like about your appearance?
What don't you like and why?**

_____

_____

_____

_____

_____

**List the ways you can begin the process of change that are
realistic for you.** Examples: Begin walking, stop eating cake,
see a nutritionist. Or maybe the process is even slower. Maybe start
by finding a gym and walking past it. Go home and make an
appointment to take a tour of the gym.

_____

_____

_____

_____

_____

NOTES

"Do you know where you're going to,
do you like the things that life is showing you,
where are you going to, do you know?"
Theme to Mahogany

CHAPTER 2

A DEEPER LOOK

Life transitions are never easy. The ground underfoot may feel less reliable, sometimes shaky or unfamiliar. Needless to say, change comes at a price, but not without opportunity.

Taking the next steps, and a deeper look inside, offers you not only insight into how you came to be, but what resources you can use as you transition into the next phase.

This chapter gives you the journaling tools to uncover the hidden feelings and unchallenged beliefs that may be holding you back. Beginning in Week Three, you will examine how your body and mind work together. In Week Four, you will tackle some of the harder questions in the section on denial. The mind/body connection and problems of denial are intricately bound together. Indeed, the body will remember what the mind chooses to forget. So in learning to listen to your body, you will also be working ahead and addressing issues that you may have tried to ignore.

Together, the exercises in Weeks Two and Three will take you deeper inside and reveal those attributes that will help bolster your transitions as well as the faults that are standing in your way. You will be one step closer to finding your naked and true self.

"Put your ear down close to your soul
and listen hard."
ANNE SEXTON

WEEK THREE

THE MIND/BODY CONNECTION

Listen. Do you hear it? Your body is talking to you right now.
Listen and it will tell you the secrets to impeccable health,
confidence and success. Listen in the same way you would listen
to a favorite teacher or the way you would listen to your car if
it made an unfamiliar sound.

You must be open and willing to expose your feelings in order to
hear what your inner self is saying. Listen and be aware.

Are you feeling tension, anxiety, or fear? Do you feel butterflies,
pain, or perhaps even joy? Learn to listen to your gut. It is your
intuition, your inner guide, and your body's gauge. It's telling you
how you're doing and if you're going in the right direction.

Once you've learned to capture the fleeting inner messages we so
often ignore, and learn to trust them, you will embark on a new
way of life that puts your higher self in charge of your destiny.
Trusting your instincts means you will have strength and mastery
over each new step.

When you make a decision, how does it feel? Do you feel good or
sick to your stomach? Your body is telling you something. Pay close
attention and *don't be afraid of what you might learn.*

Our bodies are always talking to us, but we must listen in order to hear the message. Suppose you plan to give a speech. The whole morning you are a nervous wreck. Your palms are sweating. Your heart is racing. Why? You have a fear of speaking in public. This is a fear shared by most people.

Or suppose you're taking a nice leisurely walk down the street. You meet a "friend." You exchange greetings. You engage in conversation. You say good-bye. But as you walk away, you feel uneasy and tense. Ask yourself, "What just happened in my life? Who did I just run into? Every time I run into him, I have anxiety. I wonder what it is about my connection to this person that makes me feel physically out of sorts?"

The answer is not so easy. Your response to this person is highly subjective, relating specifically to your own history with that person. To uncloak your response, you will need to consider the kinds of responses this person caused in the past, and in what context.

Your physical response is your first clue; the mindful discovery of how it came to be takes you even closer to the truth. Louise Hay, in her book, *You Can Heal Yourself*, calls this "outer effects of inner thoughts."

Our body is the vessel that carries us through life. It is comprised of far more than tissue, muscle and bone. It contains our life experiences – a valuable cargo. Just as we have behavior patterns learned from childhood, so does our body assimilate patterns of past and present experiences that result in a physical response to a situation.

If we were cared for in a loving way as infants and were fed when we cried for food and held when we needed to be comforted, we learned how to feel secure and to trust others. As we grew, we began to articulate our needs. If our caregivers responded with positive feelings, our minds received healthy messages, too.

But what if the reverse were true? Sometimes, when emotional pain is deep, the mind goes numb and the body takes over. Bad backs, ulcers, acne, thinning hair, reflux conditions and headaches are all symptoms of unmanaged stress, anxiety or suppressed emotions. In the face of stress, some of us experience no symptoms at all. Why? Because people respond differently, even in similar situations.

Still some people, for reasons of physical constitution or for a host of reasons not yet known, respond to stress in ways that will not always reflect the same symptoms. Symptom patterns help us to identify signals from the body, but people vary so much that physical responses are usually yours and yours only.

Here is an example of how the same situation can evoke different responses. Five people get onto an elevator. The elevator gets stuck between floors. One person puts on her headset, listens to music and does not care. A second person has an anxiety attack because he panics in claustrophobic situations. A third gets on the cell phone and calls for help while the fourth feels his blood pressure rising as he realizes he's going to miss his interview. The fifth sees this as an opportunity to bring new people into her life.

Every person will respond differently. To each his own experience; to each his own response.

Your body is speaking to you. Are you listening?

Here is a story about the body reacting to stress. Sherry, a 25 year-old new mother sat in my office last week and bemoaned the fact that, "Every time I have lunch with my best friend Joan, she says something demeaning and puts me down. And every time I walk away from lunch, I feel nauseous and have a headache. We've been best friends for years. We're like sisters. I don't get it."

Clearly, Joan is not good for Sherry's health. Rectifying the situation means first recognizing the pattern and then turning those feelings into something tangible. We are still exploring what it is about Joan that awakens discomfort in Sherry.

We all have friends like that. *So why do we keep seeing them?*

Why do we remain in a relationship that gives us anxiety? For starters, you can tell right away if a person doesn't make you feel good about yourself. I always ask my clients if they are dating and, if so, how they feel about themselves when they are with this person.

Everyone has the ability to be self-intuitive. In the situation where the difficult relationship is with a relative, you have fewer, and if not more difficult, choices. Say you like spending holidays with your family, except that your Aunt Sue is always there. Aunt Sue makes sarcastic remarks about your appearance, your job or your husband and you leave feeling the warmth of your other family members, but the mean sting of Aunt Sue's comments.

You know that she will always be welcome – your family will not just reject her from these occasions. And why should you avoid family functions just because of one bad attitude? The lesson here is not to let one bad apple spoil the bunch. You *have* to be together on certain occasions, but understand that it's okay for you *not* to like some of your relatives and yet still be civil to them.

If it's your parent, a mother-in-law, or a child, it becomes more complicated. You still need to protect yourself from angry energy. You have to understand that there are repercussions to other family members if you decide to respond to the toxicity that they are emitting.

Again, when it's a friend who continues to put you down, you have more choices. You may decide the friendship has other good qualities, and choose to remain friends but limit your exposure to him or her. If the redeeming qualities do not outweigh the bad, you may want to rethink the relationship altogether.

So listen to your inner self in the form of body feelings and fleeting thoughts that speak truthfully to certain situations and people. Listen, because your body knows. Even if there is no obvious reason for your reaction, no logical, formal reason for you to feel a negative response, your body is telling you something.

You owe it to yourself to listen to its wisdom. As Dr. Christian Northrop, author of *Women's Bodies, Women's Wisdom* said, "intuition is the direct perception of truth independent of any reasoning process."

Listen, learn and trust.

JOURNALING IN PRACTICE

Sherry, the new mother I mentioned previously, suffered from frequent headaches, backaches, and occasional anxiety. As a new parent, she chalked up most of her symptoms to the stress of motherhood, not an unreasonable conclusion.

Hearing Sherry talk about her relationships gave me the idea that maybe this answer was premature. Sherry used homework assignments similar to those in this section to help her identify how she harbors her feelings in her body. Each day she would make a mental note of how her body felt after seeing a friend, a neighbor, even her husband. In the evening, she recorded those feelings in a journal, along with how her body felt before, during and after the encounter.

Over the course of a few weeks, Sherri began to see a pattern in her physical responses and was able to identify that her "aches and pains" increased when she was around certain people, often because she was tensing her body, bracing herself for their "attack." Sherry also made note of how her own messages to people, both verbally and physically, contributed to her tension.

She then moved on to the harder task of deciding how she would deal with each individual situation: whether she wanted to spend less time with a particular person, whether she felt she should verbally express her feelings, or whether the benefit of the relationship outweighed her need to respond.

QUESTIONS & EXERCISES I

MIND/BODY

Illness

Your body is telling you something, whether it is about your job, a decision, a person or a situation. It is speaking to you and only to you. In order to learn and understand what it is saying, you must learn how to translate its messages so you can act upon them.

Each of us has a vulnerable part of our body, where the stress we face daily manifests itself. In many cases, we are unable to control these stresses, but in some cases, we can. The questions below are designed to help you become aware of whom or what causes you stress, and what you can and cannot change.

What illness befalls you the most? For example: Colds, headaches, backaches, migraines, asthma or insomnia.

_____

_____

_____

_____

When you feel stressed, which part of your body feels most vulnerable? Which part of your body is most affected when you feel down?

_____

_____

_____

_____

_____

The Voice Inside

I once worked with a 27-year-old woman who was in a car accident. She was shaken and tossed about. The car was totaled but she was able to walk out of the car with only a few bruises. However, she soon became incapacitated and fell into a deep depression. Her physician referred her to me. Her physical symptoms were that she had severe anxiety, was unable to move and wake up in the morning, or get out of bed. She was having nightmares unrelated to the accident. Her muscles and bones hurt her. She could not speak. She could barely move and her boyfriend basically carried her into her first session.

In order to be sure I was not misdiagnosing her, I sent her to an internist and a psychiatrist. They said that physically she was fine and the psychiatrist recommended that I continue to work with her because she felt safe with me. She was able to describe the car accident and then she started to cry. She had what appeared to be post traumatic stress disorder.

I asked her what she enjoyed doing before the accident and she said she loved writing and enjoyed success as a photographer. I asked her to keep a journal. At the top of every page, I gave the simple prompt: "Why are you feeling so sad?" followed by the question, "What is your body telling you?"

In our session I did a deep relaxation exercise with her. After this exercise, I realized that her defenses were down. I said, "Talk to your body and ask your body 'When was the last time I felt this much pain?'" She left the session and came back with ten pages of a horrific early childhood trauma that she had repressed for 23 years. The car accident, the shaking of her body and the tossing about, the suddenness, the fear – it all came flooding back to her. Her body remembered what her mind had so skillfully repressed. Now we were able to begin our work.

The next time you feel vulnerable or afraid, try to figure out what your body is saying to you. Make sure you are in a quiet place, so you can listen, uninterrupted to what your body is saying. Close your eyes and try to relax for a few minutes by breathing deeply.

Now focus on what part of our body still feels tension. Ask yourself, "When was the last time my body felt this way? When was the first time I felt this way?" Go back as far as you can. Were you five years old? Seven? Ten? Try to remember the times you felt this way. Try to track the feelings that precipitated that event.

Describe the feelings.

NOTES

QUESTIONS & EXERCISES II

DIS-EASE

Think about the word "disease." In common parlance, the word "disease" conjures dramatic images, most of which are associated with the body and physical challenge.

Now let's break the word down to its component parts: dis-ease. By breaking it down, the word means simply *not* at *ease*.

Dis-ease, as we will use it here and in keeping with its origin, can emerge from a thought, an opinion or a reaction to an outside situation. Sometimes a dis-ease is really a message in disguise.

Sometimes it is the result of another person's negative energy. Once we are able to extract the meaning behind our discomfort then perhaps we can begin to cure what ails our mind, spirit and body.

Who in your life, if anyone, causes you to feel ill at ease (or in *dis-ease*)? List them by name.

_____

_____

_____

_____

_____

In what way?

_____

_____

_____

_____

_____

What happens to you physically or emotionally when you are near each person?

_____

_____

_____

_____

_____

Has it always been this way? If not, when did this start?

_____

_____

_____

_____

_____

If it is a family member, how will you plan to make your next encounter easier?

_____

_____

_____

_____

_____

NOTES

QUESTIONS & EXERCISES III

VULNERABILITY

What is vulnerability? When you're vulnerable, you're naked to the elements. Being vulnerable, you are susceptible to personal injury, attack, criticism or censure. Are you vulnerable in certain situations?

What situations make you feel most vulnerable?

_____

_____

_____

_____

_____

If you know you are going into a vulnerable situation, what steps can you take so you don't have the same outcome? List the concrete things you are going to do before this situation next occurs.

_____

_____

_____

_____

_____

NOTES

QUESTIONS & EXERCISES IV

FRIENDS

Sometimes messages come to you when you are with certain friends. Your body is telling you whether or not they are good for your soul and your health. Some people are toxic and make you feel vulnerable and *in dis-ease*. It may simply be a friend's own vulnerability that makes you feel what you feel about him or her. It is important to identify who these people are and listen to what your body is saying about them.

List three friends with whom you spend the most time. How do you feel after you see each of these friends? For example: Rebecca has been friends with Susan for many years. Susan always finds ways of reminding Rebecca of Rebecca's past traumas and broken relationships, all in the name of "friendship." Rebecca seems to handle the conversation just fine until the next day when she wakes up with a migraine.

_____

_____

_____

_____

_____

Here is a little chart you can use to help you connect your illness to the situation or person who precipitated it. Follow the examples and add your own.

Person or event	Symptoms you experience
ex-husband or ex-boyfriend	nausea, fear, anxiety
trusted friend	safety, happiness, vitality

Do you see a pattern? Half the battle is feeling that you have a sense of control over the situation. And as long as you are cognizant of the pattern, you can deal with it because it becomes predictable. Remember: forewarned is forearmed.

Once you have become aware of what is happening and how you are feeling, you can decide how to manage the situation. Example: Rebecca decides to remove Susan from her social circle.

EFFECTS

What situation has the most effect on you in a positive or negative way? What is your "gut" saying about those situations? Can you translate what your body is telling you? Can you identify which situations are better for you than others?

How does your job/school make you feel physically?

_____

_____

_____

_____

_____

How do you "feel" about those with whom you work/study?

_____

_____

_____

_____

_____

What can you do to rectify what you feel without changing your job/school?

_____

_____

_____

_____

_____

Are you doing what "feels right?" This is a broad question, but when directed toward your physical self, the answer can be quite powerful. How are you working towards your purpose?

_____

_____

_____

_____

_____

Based on your discovery of body responses: If you are in the workforce, is it worth changing jobs? Think about this and write your thoughts.

_____

_____

_____

_____

_____

NOTES

QUESTIONS & EXERCISES V

BE PREPARED

It helps to be prepared. Remember the feeling of meeting someone on the street and when he or she walks away, you think, "Wow, I wish I had said _____ "?

Well, now is your chance. Your body is a barometer. But you have to be your own "self-meteorologist." You have to know when to take your umbrella with you. Who takes your umbrella away when it starts to rain?

With whom do you feel the most vulnerable or unprotected? Describe the feeling.

_____

_____

_____

_____

_____

Try to remember and write about a situation where you didn't say what you should have, and how what you didn't say affected the outcome:

_____

_____

_____

_____

_____

You have all the answers within you and all you need to do is learn to listen to the response. Can you learn to listen to the answer without analyzing or reasoning with it?

Write about a situation that troubles you:

_____

_____

_____

_____

_____

Now, without thinking, write from your gut the solution to this problem.

_____

_____

_____

_____

_____

NOTES

"Facts do not cease to exist because they are ignored."
ALDOUS HUXLEY

WEEK FOUR

DENIAL

Are you facing your true and naked self, with all its faults and attributes? This is probably the most difficult task you will have to face – to uncover the things about yourself that you deny.

Each of us has a part of us that we choose, consciously or not, to keep hidden. Denial is a defense mechanism we use to hide certain truths that have happened in our life because they seem too difficult. Sometimes we have unfounded fears that are deeply hidden or we have experienced specific events that caused us trauma.

Perhaps we have had a tragic experience that we have buried far back in our subconsciousness. By denying that these events have ever happened, we protect ourselves from the pain of reality. That behavior of repressing these feelings deep within yourself finds ways of creeping through your pores and affecting your body and behavior. I believe that *our bodies remember what our minds choose to forget.*

As you move past denial, it will likely mark an intense period of growth. I do not think that these exercises will lift the veil of every hidden secret within you. They will start you on your way to uncovering the sometimes painful truths that prevent you from moving forward.

The pain one feels as one moves beyond denial is inevitable. Approaching this pain with determination and pushing away fear will bring you closer to your naked self, your true self.

Remember, your true self holds the wisdom of who you are, and where you are going. The secrets you keep are like poison – so get rid of them. Painful as it might be, moving past denial is an essential step towards self-awareness.

Give yourself room to think and relax during this process. Resist the urge to be judgmental. There's no need to be harsh with yourself or to others. The process you are about to embark upon requires a level of honesty that may seem unfamiliar, difficult and even frightening at times.

Overcoming denial requires strength. You will have to lift the boulders that block your way. In the process, you will learn how to accept responsibility for your own life. This is a watershed moment in your personal growth – and you will find that it is worth the risks.

Masks and Shadows

Sometimes people in denial will adopt a "mask" in order to disguise themselves from the rest of the world. They become a chameleon, behaving in a way they believe will please the persons they are with, changing affect on demand. Quite often, denial runs so deep that they are unaware of its existence. In fact, they may not even recognize themselves if they looked in the mirror.

Of course, you may be wondering: If my life is going along just fine, why should I want to know if I'm in denial? Why not let sleeping dogs lie?

But *there*, as Shakespeare would say, *is the rub*. Denial may seem hidden, but in fact, it tip-toes out every so often and sneaks up on us. That is when we start experiencing ailments such as stomachaches, headaches and backaches, as we learned in Week Three.

Denial can be responsible for negative emotions such as sarcasm, fits of anger, aggressive behavior and sullen moods. Denial can also lead to addiction to drugs, food or sex.

It takes a good detective to unearth denial, and sometimes *we* are the only detective we have. We are the only ones who can move the blocks neatly stacked in front of our hidden-most secrets.

No doubt, we deny certain realities in our lives because they are too "dark" to deal with. We tell ourselves that pain of memory cuts too close to the bone. We cannot afford to neglect our dark side. It will haunt us, it will stop us, and it will prevent us from being a whole person.

The Swiss psychologist Carl Jung coined the phrase *shadow work*. He believed that in order to live healthy, complete lives we have to embrace our negative as well as positive thoughts, our dreams as well as our hidden demons.

How do we lure the shadow from its hidden place? Slowly at first, so as not to frighten ourselves with whatever it is that we have so carefully hidden.

Take your life in your own hands and what happens?
A terrible thing! No one to blame."
ERICA JONG

A Camouflaged Life

Another important facet of denial involves "*mask wearing.*" The object is to prevent recognition of our true identity by those from whom we are hiding, including, on occasion, ourselves. Perhaps we fear others might find something about us that they will not like. The longer we wear the mask, the harder it is to remove.

We begin to live a camouflaged life. After awhile, we will not recognize ourselves. We cannot feel who we are. We lose ourselves and we become the mask.

In dealing with denial in the exercises that follow, I want you to take a practical approach. Remember that these exercises are *your* exercises, to be shared with whomever you want (or no one as the case may be). You can take these exercises to whatever point feels right for you. I encourage you to push yourself, but I do not believe that every detail of your inner workings must be laid bare before you can make progress. Think of it as taking away the blocks that are crowding you. Taking away only one block is measurable progress.

By opening the windows and letting the negative energy out, you are creating a space, a psychic place to grow.

"The only difference between stumbling blocks and steppingstones is the way in which we use them."
UNKNOWN

JOURNALING IN PRACTICE

At 28, Mindy had begun to distance herself emotionally from her three-year-old daughter. Although still attentive to all of her daughter's physical needs, Mindy felt herself pulling away when it came to the more subtle, emotional needs of her child.

The prospect of not being the best mother she could be for her daughter gave Mindy terrible anxiety. She had no idea why this was happening. Her life, in every way she could see, was in good order. She had a solid marriage and everyone was healthy.

I gave Mindy journaling homework specifically to look for missing pieces from the past, first asking her to draw images of her childhood family and later having her identify some of the feelings attached to those images. I asked her to write about family secrets, however minor they seemed. Mindy held back for a few weeks, drawing pictures as she thought they were "supposed" to be.

I asked her to bring photos from her childhood. She noticed that her mom was not present in any of the photos. Now the pictures she drew began to change. Mindy's mother disappeared from the drawings. Where did she go?

Over the weeks that followed, we both learned that Mindy's mother had suffered a "breakdown" and spent months in a hospital when Mindy was only three years old. At a vulnerable age, Mindy had felt abandoned, but it wasn't until she identified these feelings 25 years later, by writing them down, that she could understand how she had distanced herself from the experience almost completely.

Now that she had her own daughter, she held a persistent fear that she too, would need to abandon her daughter, that she was slated for her own "breakdown." Mindy's fears were not at all warranted, but the shadows of the past weighed heavily on her adult life. She had begun to distance herself from her daughter in order to protect her child from the "inevitable" abandonment.

Nothing could have been further from the truth. Mindy's anxiety marked a turning point – her courage to unmask what was hidden inside allowed her to see her own fear. In time, Mindy moved through her anxiety and felt confident again in being the parent she wanted to become.

QUESTIONS & EXERCISES I

DENIAL

Try to focus on a situation that you think you may be in denial about, no matter how farfetched it may seem to you. You are probably thinking, *how do I ask a question about something I don't know?*

This is where the mind/body connection can give you clues. Look back over the previous weeks' exercises and see if there are passages that you wrote that feel odd, out of place, or not yet resolved. Think about when you were younger. Let your mind wander and see where it takes you.

Write these thoughts down on a piece of paper and look at it and ask yourself: Does this feel right? Let these thoughts sink in and see what flows in a day or a week later. See what other words come from those written words. See what associations there are.

Start slowly. Don't make the mistake of telling yourself, *"Okay, I'm going to deal with this now. I'm going to put my boots on and walk right through the mud."* Say instead, *"I'm going to put my foot outside and just test the waters."* Imagine instead that you are standing on the shoreline, watching the waves, and you say, *"I'm just going to get my toe wet to see how cold the water is."* Don't go swimming yet. It might be too deep. Just start by listening to the ocean and walking toward the shore.

For those who struggle with denying their feelings, the greatest fear is that if they touch their pain, they will start crying and never stop. That is part of the difficulty of this chapter and why it is so important that you take time to think before answering these questions. Remember, this is *your* journey, and the object is to make you *self* aware. You are getting acquainted with your true and naked self. Enjoy and nurture this relationship, because it is the most important connection we can ever make.

Breaking through the walls of denial makes room for you to love, give and create. This is the time for you to start the process of becoming the most that you can be.

EXERCISE IN DENIAL AWARENESS
Pretend that everyone in your family has come to your house.
In the space provided, draw a table and place the name of each
family member over a seat. Okay, now look around you.
Who is sitting at the table?

With whom do you feel most comfortable? Why?

_____

_____

_____

_____

_____

**With whom do you feel most uncomfortable and why do you
feel uncomfortable with that person?**

_____

_____

_____

_____

_____

What has that person done to make you feel so uptight?

_____

_____

_____

_____

_____

Do you have family secrets? What are they and how long have you kept these secrets inside yourself?

_____

_____

_____

_____

Where inside you are these secrets hiding? In your head, your stomach, your back? Where do you feel pain when you peek at one of these secrets?

_____

_____

_____

_____

_____

Who in your family has caused you shame? Do they know they have hurt you? Have you ever told them?

_____

_____

_____

_____

_____

Do they deny hurting you? Yes? No? **If yes, how does their denial affect you?**

_____

_____

_____

_____

_____

How do you express your sadness or anger? Do you cry? Do you get angry? Do you stop talking? Do you take drugs?

_____

_____

_____

_____

_____

Write down your secret.

_____

_____

_____

_____

_____

NOTES

> "The center that I cannot find is known to my unconscious mind."
> W. H. AUDEN

QUESTIONS & EXERCISES II

THINK

The following questions are not easy. If you need to go for a walk outside, this might be a good time and it might also be a good time to put on your favorite music and relax or just sit quietly. Keep breathing.

If you believe that you were neglected as a child, how does that inner belief affect the person that you are today?

_____

_____

_____

_____

_____

How would you have liked to have been treated?

_____

_____

_____

_____

_____

How do the choices you currently make in your life reflect your earlier experiences? Do you choose partners who treat you as other family members treated you?

_____

_____

_____

_____

_____

Think. Breathe. Write. Who reminds you of your past?
Write down their names. (For example: Steve reminds me of mom. Susan reminds me of my sister. Yvette- reminds me of dad.)

_____

_____

_____

_____

_____

You might be saying to yourself, _"I know. I understand why feeling past pain is important in the here and now, but that pain creates blocks inside of me."_ Please continue, because answering these questions is important.

What is your greatest fear?

_____

_____

_____

_____

How do you deal with that fear?

_____

_____

_____

_____

_____

How have you learned to cope?

_____

_____

_____

_____

_____

How has your coping style worked or not worked for you?

_____

_____

_____

_____

_____

Who do you trust to help you now?

_____

_____

_____

_____

_____

"Surround yourself with people who respect and treat you well."
CLAUDIA BLACK

In the space below, draw a picture of a table. Now put all the people with whom you feel safe around you. Who is sitting at this table? Where are you sitting?

NOTES

"The truth is that our finest moments are most likely to occur
when we are feeling deeply uncomfortable, unhappy or unfulfilled.
For it is only in such moments, propelled by our discomfort,
that we are likely to step out of our ruts and start searching
for different ways or truer answers."
M. SCOTT PECK

CHAPTER 3

TAKE INVENTORY

Imagine you are moving to a new house or apartment. You will need
to pack books and photos, dishes and clothes. You will also need to
pull out everything from the back of the closet.

Before you can move, before you can pack those boxes, you will also
need to take inventory of your possessions. You will want to make
sure to take those items that are useful and get rid of the things
that you no longer need.

Life transitions are not so different. Before you can move ahead (to a
new home, better relationships, a fresh outlook), you must first see
what you have and what you want to take with you on your journey.

In Week Five of this chapter, you will take stock of both the strengths
that propel you forward, as well as the weaknesses that are holding
you back. In Week Six, you will examine your support system – the
network of people in your life who create positive influences.

These are your "movers." They will help you move forward in your
life, be there for you in times of need, and help you realize your
goals and ambitions.

"In the middle of difficulty lies opportunity."
ALBERT EINSTEIN

WEEK FIVE

STRENGTHS AND WEAKNESSES

Strength and weakness come from the same source – deep in the core of your soul. In uncovering the outer layers of everyday life and getting acquainted with your naked self, you will begin to discover what gives you strength, as well as how that strength is challenged.

What are your strengths? Did you have to think about the answer? How fast did it come to you? Now, think about your weaknesses. Which is easier to define? Most people have no problem identifying their weaknesses, but are generally embarrassed to articulate their strengths.

Being conscious of both your strengths and weaknesses is the only way to invite meaningful change. We will ask these questions again later, but first let's examine the types of strengths and weaknesses.

Identifying Strengths

True inner strength is an intimate surge of energy that helps you persevere each day with commitment and patience. *Inner* strength is about being self-aware, honest and open with your self. It is about assessing what you need to move forward and taking the appropriate steps to get you where you want to go. When you think about your strengths, think about the successes you have had in different aspects of your life and your ability to reach specific goals.

Like a muscle, inner strength is not built overnight; it requires practice and endurance. Just as you would go to a gym or lift weights to build muscles, inner strength has its own program. Inner strength requires us to stay connected and attuned to the rhythms of others and also remain keenly aware of who we are and how we perceive our goals. Inner strength cannot be built on the opinions of others; it develops only from hard work on our part, building confidence daily, persevering in our goals.

Strengths can also be more tangible. Musical and artistic talent, carpentry skills, mathematical ability, gardening know-how, a keen eye for detail, perhaps even the capacity to be a friend – all strengths and resources from which to grow.

These more practical sources of strength are the basis from which inner strength will emerge. When you do the work, strength in one area has a magical power to generate even more strength.

Identifying Weaknesses

Weaknesses are easier to define for most people. When you think about your weaknesses, think of any behavior that prevents you from moving forward and gets in the way of what you want to achieve. Here is a list of some of the more common weaknesses I have seen in my practice:

• Not standing up for yourself
• Being overly self-deprecating
• Being dishonest
• Holding on to anger
• Not taking responsibility for your own behavior
• Procrastinating
• Being too controlling or allowing yourself to be controlled
• Putting others down in order to feel better about yourself

What all of these have in common is an element of fear. If you have trouble standing up for yourself, you likely fear the outcome of what you really want to say. If you put yourself down in front of others, perhaps you are afraid of your *real* potential.

If you are dishonest, there is certainly a fear of the truth. As we continue down the list, we see that fear is at the root of each of these behaviors. Facing these fears has a powerful effect and the inevitable change that follows all too often reveals how these "weaknesses" can actually become our strengths.

Transformations

Knowing your strengths and weaknesses arms you with self-knowledge and transformative power. Facing fears headlong disempowers the fear itself; it can no longer hold you back.

In the movie, *Sleeping with the Enemy*, Julia Roberts plays an abused housewife who escapes the wrath of her tyrannical husband. In a staged boating accident, her character escapes by swimming to safety. She had always been afraid of the water, but in her plan to leave her husband, she secretly learned to swim, at once overcoming the fear of the water and making way to overcome her fear of leaving.

The character slowly built her strength, physically and emotionally prior to her escape. Her fear of drowning symbolized her emotional fear. Once she learned that she could swim, that she could do something she thought she could never ever do, she felt a sense of power to embark on an even tougher goal – to leave a terrible and oppressive situation.

Here are exercises and questions to help you define your strengths and weaknesses. Once your awareness increases, you will see how your strengths will help you overcome any weaknesses that stand in your way.

> "Man is ultimately self-determining."
> VICTOR E. FRANKEL

QUESTIONS & EXERCISES I

LIST YOUR STRENGTHS

Listing your strengths is a form of affirmation. It confirms what you know to be true and marks a starting point from which you will continue to build. You will list strengths in the present tense (as in "I am") and recite them daily. You are accentuating and articulating the positive and reminding yourself of your gifts.

This is an extremely important part of the journaling process and you may even continue doing this long after the other exercises are finished. You can even keep adding to your list of strengths as you go along. You may not have discovered some of them yet.

Write a list of ten of your strengths on a small piece of paper or on an index card. Fold the paper or card and keep it in your wallet. Look at it periodically throughout the day.

Put a copy of your list on your refrigerator to remind yourself on a daily basis of just how strong you are. As you open the fridge, read the list of strengths to yourself or say them out aloud. Don't hesitate to add to the list at any given time. Be generous and be kind to yourself.

NOTES

QUESTIONS & EXERCISES II

ANALYZE YOUR STRENGTHS

What is a strength? A "strength" is the quality, state or property of being strong; it is the power to resist force, stress or wear; the power to resist attack; firmness or toughness.

What makes you strong? What makes you durable? What makes you powerful? What qualities about yourself do you champion? What makes you a winner? Think about these strengths and remember them.

Write your list of 10 strengths here. For example: I'm a people person, I can make people feel comfortable around me.

_____

_____

_____

_____

_____

_____

_____

_____

_____

_____

_____

How have these strengths helped you in the past?

_____

_____

_____

_____

_____

Perhaps you have unique gifts and talents that you might not realize are your strengths. What are your unique gifts and talents?

_____

_____

_____

_____

_____

If you were put on this earth to serve a specific purpose, what would that purpose be?

_____

_____

_____

_____

_____

What can you do with your talents that would help others?

_____

_____

_____

_____

_____

How can you use these strengths to help you achieve what you want in the future?

_____

_____

_____

_____

_____

Who in your family nurtured your strengths?

_____

_____

_____

_____

_____

How did they do this?

_____

_____

_____

_____

_____

Are the strengths you see and feel the same as the ones your family thinks you have? In what way?

_____

_____

_____

_____

_____

NOTES

QUESTIONS & EXERCISES III

WEAKNESSES

What is a weakness? A weakness is defined as a lack of strength or energy or insufficient intellect, character, strength or will power. By recognizing your weaknesses, you are learning about your naked self.

Armed with this knowledge, you can begin to overcome your weaknesses and learn from them. It is only when you identify what is lacking that you can begin to fill the void.

What do you perceive as your weaknesses?

_____

_____

_____

_____

_____

List them in the order of which they are most difficult for you to deal with.

_____

_____

_____

_____

_____

How do your weaknesses hinder your goals and your life's purpose?

_____

_____

_____

_____

_____

How have these protected you?

_____

_____

_____

_____

What have they protected you from? For example: A woman who is slightly overweight and complains that she can't find a date because she perceives that men only want to be with "thin women." Her fear of dating propels her to keep eating, because it is easier for her to be heavy than to be judged in a dating situation.

_____

_____

_____

_____

Who in your family nurtured your weaknesses, not enabling you to meet healthy challenges? How did they do this?

_____

_____

_____

_____

_____

NOTES

> "I shut my eyes in order to see."
> PAUL GAUGUIN

QUESTIONS & EXERCISES IV

CHANGING WEAKNESSES INTO STRENGTHS

Is it truly possible to transform weakness into strength, you may wonder? The good news is that once you've acknowledged your weaknesses, you can move forward.

The process of change always begins with knowledge. You are taking an intelligent approach to a difficult but rewarding process. Go slowly through the questions and be thoughtful and patient.

Which weaknesses can you change?

_____

_____

_____

_____

What's stopped you from changing them?

_____

_____

_____

_____

_____

What can you do to change your weaknesses?

_____

_____

_____

_____

_____

Who can you enlist to help you?

_____

_____

_____

_____

_____

Where do you think your weaknesses come from?

_____

_____

_____

_____

_____

How long do you intend to hold on to them? Why?

_____

_____

_____

_____

_____

NOTES

QUESTIONS & EXERCISES V

ANALYZING YOUR STRENGTHS *AND* WEAKNESSES
The key to success in life is finding out what you are good at – and what
you are not good at – and then applying that knowledge to your career,
family and relationships.

**Are your professional strengths different from your personal
strengths? How?**

_____

_____

_____

_____

_____

List your professional strengths.

_____

_____

_____

_____

_____

What qualities do people at work or school respect about you?

_____

_____

_____

_____

_____

What do you think people at work or school don't like about you?

_____

_____

_____

_____

_____

Do you see these traits as strengths or weaknesses?

_____

_____

_____

_____

_____

How can you use your strengths to enhance your work?

_____

_____

_____

_____

_____

NOTES

QUESTIONS & EXERCISES VI

TRANSFORMATION

Transformation is the process of change. It is means to markedly alter or convert the appearance or form of something. This is what you are now doing – your transformation to a new self is now underway.

By recognizing your strengths and weaknesses, you begin the process of shedding your old clothes, like a butterfly emerging from its cocoon.

Answer the questions below and witness the transformation.

List five ways you can change your weaknesses into strengths.
For example: I'm afraid of speaking in public and I'm an attorney. I'll enroll in a public speaking class. Once I've learned effective public speaking, I'll help others do the same. I'll challenge my fear not only in the way it is holding me back, but also to become the mirror of my future strength by helping others overcome this
same problem.

_____

_____

_____

_____

_____

NOTES

"A dwarf standing on the shoulders of a giant
may see farther than a giant himself."
ROBERT BURTON

WEEK SIX

SUPPORT SYSTEMS

When I was seven years old, I went to Camp Maple Lake in Livingston Manor, New York. We had a theme song and it went like this: *Friends, friends, friends, we will always be: whether in fair or in dark stormy weather, Camp Maple Lake will keep us together.* This chapter is about friendship, relationships, buddies and support systems.

In the chapter on self-esteem, we heralded the importance of independence. But there are times when we need, and indeed, *want*, others around us. To keep life in balance, we need a good sense of self and autonomy *and* we need people in our lives with whom to share our experiences.

Humans are social beings. So it is no surprise that they thrive when they have good relationships. People thrive when they have strong support networks. But support has to be mutual. This means knowing how to ask for help when you need it and how to give it as well.

Negotiating Support

Asking for support is not always easy. For those with a strong sense of independence, which is usually a strong asset, it can be difficult not only to ask for support but also to accept it. Those who have trouble articulating their needs, or those who feel others should intuit their needs, are particularly vulnerable to not getting support when they need it.

If this is a problem for you, remember that no one, other than you, can read your mind. If you need help and support from a friend, spouse or parent and he or she is not aware of it, it is your responsibility to let him or her know your needs.

When asking for support, it is crucial to be specific and zero in on exactly what it is that you want. This is a good time to practice positive listening and responding skills. If you are asking for support, you need to ask for it in a positive and constructive manner.

Being critical of what someone is doing *wrong* is less likely to be effective. For example, if you feel your husband or wife, boyfriend or girlfriend, neglects actively listening to you, you need to tell him or her exactly how to *improve* rather than what he or she is doing wrong.

"Why don't you ever listen to me? How can I talk to you with the TV on?" has a combative tone (and they are also questions and not statements.) But *"I need you to listen to what I have to say about _____"* or *"I need ten minutes of your undivided attention"* are more specific and both leave out criticism.

Your spouse or partner is a valuable support person, but no matter how close you are, you may need to ask directly for what you want. He or she is unlikely to know what you are thinking unless you say so. The clearer you are about your needs, the better the chance of getting the support you seek.

When it comes to relationships, particularly romantic ones, try to maintain balance in giving and receiving support. Reciprocity is achievable, but it doesn't necessarily mean an "equal" exchange based on one partner's interpretation.

What may seem like support for one person may be wasted effort for another. This is why being specific and clear, particularly with your partner, will help both of you maintain a mutually supportive atmosphere.

As John Gray states so succinctly in *Men Are from Mars, Women Are from Venus:* "We're from different planets. We'll never have the same needs." In fact, we don't have to give each other the same thing. But we do have to give each other the same quality of effort.

If he wants time alone, then you have to be willing to respect that and if you want more quality time, you should get it as well.

Support or Baggage: How to Know the Difference
In this section, you will locate and define your support network. Like the previous exercises, it may not be as simple as counting the familiar and smiling faces you see everyday. You will likely need to take a closer look.

As you open up to your true self, your naked self, you will also become more intimate with your own needs, dreams and goals. Whatever transition you are making in your life, your success is held partly in the hands of those around you.

You have to trust those helping hands, but first you must know the difference between a hand that reaches out to you and a hand that takes from you.

There are people in our lives who, at the end of a phone conversation or a dinner date, leave us feeling depleted of energy, wishing we had not answered the phone or gone out to dinner at all. We all know such people. They love to put others down, elevating themselves in the process.

They thrive on your bad news. They dish the dirt on anyone else's bad news because it makes them feel good. When they call, they are itching to hear your problems, whatever they are, so they can turn them back on you.

Why don't we walk away from those people immediately? What are we getting from staying in a relationship with them? Why do we keep people in our lives who aren't supportive? We may call these people our "friends." They may even be relatives.

Just because they are familiar does not mean they need to be part of our support network. We have seen how these people can make us feel physically ill. When deciding on who your support network will be, reconsider feelings that were identified in earlier exercises.

In the exercises that follow, you will be asked to look at what you value in your relationships. This will help you determine how best to create, or recreate, a support network suited to your needs and goals.

Your naked self has the innate wisdom to know what is best for you. As you tap into that wisdom, you will begin to notice that your true self is gravitating toward others who facilitate, rather than eradicate, this part of you.

As you identify your support network, or who will be part of your team, think of yourself as a top ranked athlete. You need a coach, a doctor, a trainer and a physical therapist, among others.

As a highly ranked competitor, you are certain of your talents and feel those talents deserve to be nurtured by the best. Why would you choose members for your support team who envy your talents and attempt to undermine your goals?

You know you deserve the best, so you seek the best. By the same token, reciprocity in this situation means that you share your good fortune and talents with those who support you. When you win the gold medal, acknowledge it as a team effort and reward your supporters as they have rewarded you.

Whatever your gold medal – be it a new career, a fulfilling relationship or overcoming an obstacle – make it no secret that you are bringing along only those worthy of a unique and valuable journey.

JOURNALING IN PRACTICE

Gina, an actor, came to me because she wasn't getting enough work. A beautiful young woman with ample training and experience, a top agent, and a seemingly good attitude, there seemed to be no apparent reason for her stalled career. Gina and her agent had become close friends and as friends will do, Gina disclosed much about her private life to the agent. Gina trusted this woman with her career – even her secrets. Not long after Gina came to me, she discovered that directors were passing on her for parts because of negative comments made by the agent herself. Gina was furious and rightfully so. Problem solved. Gina had a bad agent. But the story does not end there.

As Gina described her relationship with her agent-friend, it became apparent that Gina had been getting "clues" from the agent all along – clues that perhaps this woman was no one's friend, particularly Gina's. The agent, it seemed, liked to "fish for information," only to use that information against Gina.

The agent apparently was envious of Gina's boldness in seeking a career as an actor – something the agent wanted for herself. I asked Gina to keep a journal describing the qualities of all the people in her life, including family, friends, and colleagues, and to note whether they'd been supportive or not. Gina made detailed notes; her sense of betrayal by the agent spurring her to go deeper.

Gina was a bold woman who had, years before, distanced herself from her own mother because she was what Gina called "a busybody gossip." She, too, had betrayed Gina's trust on more than one occasion. Even though Gina limited her contact with her mother, she effectively substituted the negative behavior of her mother by unwittingly choosing her agent, who had the same pattern of behavior. Gina's writing gave her written evidence to see the qualities she found familiar, harmful as they were, and a very good reason to reexamine her support network.

"If we don't change, we don't grow.
If we don't grow we are not really living.
Growth demands a temporary surrender of security."
GAIL SHEEHY

QUESTIONS & EXERCISES I

Sometimes familiarity feels comfortable and we don't question it. As you do the exercises, keep in mind that seeing the positive and negative in what seems familiar can be a challenge, just as we saw in earlier sections. Familiarity may be predictable and thus seductive, but it is not necessarily what is best for you.

EXPECTATIONS
**Are your expectations of people and situations too high?
Do you know them well enough to have their unconditional support, or, have you been pleasantly surprised by those around you?**

_____

_____

_____

_____

_____

What qualities do you look for in a friendship? Are these the same ones you would look for in a relationship with a husband or wife?

_____

_____

_____

_____

_____

How does what you expect from a friend differ from what you expect from a husband, wife, lover, life-partner?

_____

_____

_____

_____

_____

Remember when you were younger and thought about the qualities of a life mate? List the qualities you wanted then.

_____

_____

_____

_____

_____

List the qualities you want now.

_____

_____

_____

_____

_____

List the specific qualities of the person with whom you are currently in a relationship.

_____

_____

_____

_____

_____

NOTES

QUESTIONS & EXERCISES II

SUPPORT

Support comes in all forms – emotional, financial, professional and physical. It could be some or all of the above. But one thing is certain. As human beings, we cannot live alone.

We are part of the tapestry of life and each of us is an interwoven thread. Together, we create a functioning society and the foundation of a family.

What does being supported by someone mean to you?

Who has been supportive of you in the past? List friends, relatives, siblings, teachers, professors, others and tell how each was supportive.

Your Support System
Learn to trust your inner wisdom for guidance. That guidance comes from a matrix of family and friends who care about you. Who in your life supports you now?

List the person	How is she or he supportive?

List three people whom you feel have been supportive of you from the time you were a child.

_____

_____

_____

_____

_____

What do you like about the type of support you received?

_____

_____

_____

_____

_____

Does the support you received enable you to feel good about yourself or does it cause you conflict? In what way?

_____

_____

_____

_____

_____

NOTES

QUESTIONS & EXERCISES III

Helping or Hindering?

Many people recreate their family structure through the people they choose to ask for support. In seeking support, you may be asking people who can actually hinder you because of their own needs and insecurities. Here is where you must follow your inner wisdom to help you determine the difference.

Have family members' support helped you or hindered you? In what way has their support helped you?

_____

_____

_____

_____

_____

In what way has it hindered you?

_____

_____

_____

_____

_____

Who supports you, but with a price? What is that support?

_____

_____

_____

_____

_____

What is the price? Is it worth it?

_____

_____

_____

_____

_____

Who are the best people that you can surround yourself with? Why?

_____

_____

_____

_____

_____

NOTES

QUESTIONS & EXERCISES IV

WHOM DO YOU SUPPORT?

As with the rhythm of life, there is ebb and flow, give and take. But it is important to have boundaries. Recognize those who take your support yet leave you feeling drained. Also recognize when it is your turn to be the support, the hand that reaches out, the rock solid friend.

List the people to whom you have given support.

_____

_____

_____

_____

_____

How did you support them? What did you give to them emotionally, physically, and/or spiritually?

_____

_____

_____

_____

_____

Did they appreciate your support? How did they express their gratitude?

_____

_____

_____

_____

_____

NOTES

QUESTIONS & EXERCISES V

STRINGS ATTACHED

When those who support you ask for immediate returns on their investment, it may not always be worth it. Are these people jealous, competitive, emotionally lacking or just selfish?

Compassion and understanding are qualities we seek in those who promise their unconditional support. Think about those around you and the effect they have on your well-being.

Do you keep people in your life, even when they don't support you? Why don't you walk away from those people? What are you getting from them?

_____

_____

_____

_____

_____

When you are with them, or when you leave them, how do you feel? Have they sapped your energy? Given you energy?

_____

_____

_____

_____

_____

Who has supported you without strings attached?

_____

_____

_____

_____

_____

Who is in your support system now?

_____

_____

_____

_____

_____

Do you surround yourself with people who enrich your life? Do they help you feel great about who you are? Or do they make you feel sad to be you? Name the people who make you feel good about yourself.

_____

_____

_____

_____

_____

**Name the people you would like to have as part of
your support system, but you haven't the courage to
get close to them.**

_____

_____

_____

_____

_____

What qualities draw you to these people?

_____

_____

_____

_____

_____

What can you do to bring them into your life?

_____

_____

_____

_____

_____

Many people recreate their family structure by choosing certain people to be part of their lives. Are you maintaining the patterns of your childhood? How?

_____

_____

_____

_____

_____

These answers might cause you to do some house cleaning with friendships that do not work for you. As you reread your lists of friends and support systems, takers and givers, you will have greater clarity as to who is and is not good for you. It may be time to sweep away the cobwebs.

Remember, you are moving on with your life. The inventory has been taken. Now it's up to you to decide what you will bring along and what you are going to leave behind.

NOTES

"You may be disappointed if you fail,
but you are doomed if you don't try."
BEVERLY SILLS

CHAPTER 4

NEW BEGINNINGS

This chapter marks a turning point – a new beginning. You've
traveled through dark waters; you've asked difficult questions.
You've taken stock of what is past, what is present; you've
acknowledged what holds you back, and what pushes you forward.

But now you have arrived at the springtime of your journey, where
the ground below is fertile with possibility.

As you work through this and the next chapter, you will awaken
your goals and ambitions, your dreams and desires. You will also
look at how you can make your goals and dreams come to life.
You may have written down your goals and dreams before, but
perhaps they seemed too distant or difficult.

Our aim here is to take those goals and dreams and break them
down, so that you have a plan, a roadmap for getting from point A
to point D, finding the missing points B and C in between.

"Success breeds success." Your journal is your first success. What you have written in your journal so far is powerful evidence of your efforts to succeed. It is the foundation from which you will build, day by day, moment by moment if necessary, to take your true self to the landscape of your dreams.

Before we move on, take a moment and congratulate yourself. You deserve it. Take a long, deep breath and reflect on your success in reaching this point.

"I'm not afraid of storms, for I'm learning to sail my ship."
LOUISA MAY ALCOTT

WEEK SEVEN

AWAKEN YOUR DREAMS

Discovery

Sit quietly and meditate for a moment on what you desire, what you want. Pay attention, because your desires are within you, waiting for you. Listen.

What is your ultimate goal in this lifetime? What would you like to achieve? What is your ultimate dream and is this dream your purpose? Your inner guide knows why you were put on this earth. You have already peeled away some of those layers. Now, it is time for you to listen – listen to your naked self, listen to your soul's deepest desires.

Everyone's goals and dreams are different. Mine was always to be doing work that I love. You, on the other hand, might have the goal of finding the right husband or wife, or getting married before a certain age, or having kids and living in a terrific home. Someone else may want to write the "Great American Novel," have a successful business, or master the piano.

The exercises in this section are not simply about "considering your options." This is about opening yourself to possibility, allowing those rumblings inside of you to surface.

"Nothing is too good to be true."
"Nothing is too wonderful to happen"
"Nothing is too good to last."
FLORENCE SCOVEL SHINN, *The Game of Life*

Everyone has a dream, whether acknowledged or not. Some choose to ignore their dream, dismissing it as improbable. Others spend their life chasing it. And then there are those who make their dream come true. How was it actually possible for them?

Dreams are less tangible than goals. Goals are specific steps toward a measurable end, but a dream is something distant and may seem out of reach. It is a fantasy, a mental image that feels right for you, something you see for yourself that is synchronous with your world. Imagine how it must feel to realize a dream, to be doing what you love, to be sharing life with the person you feel is perfect for you, to be the friend or parent you always wanted to be.

It all starts with a dream. Everything around you is born of a dream or a vision.

Success stories often read like fairy tales, one success leading to another. When you listen to successful people talk about their journey, they will often say that they began with an intangible concept, such as an idea of the kind of person they wanted to be.

They did not start out fettered by material goals per se, but took a longer view of how their talents and skills could be part of a world they wanted to build for themselves.

It is like looking through a camera lens, widening the angle to take in a broader landscape. If the lens is focused too closely at first, you will not be able to see what you need; you will see only the smallest of pictures.

Once the broader view is in focus, you can see more clearly all the parts of the picture – all the elements you will need to see your dream realized.

The Reality of Dreams

Of course, if the picture of your life is very large, it means that hard work lies ahead. Think again of the success stories of people like Nobel Prize winners, Olympic athletes and those who lead in their field.

When we read or hear about them in the news, we see and hear success after success. But read and listen between those lines for a moment, where the struggles and failures often go untold.

I once knew a very successful entrepreneur who told me he had failed in business three times before his last company was successful. How many times do you think the Olympic gymnast fell off the balance beam before she was able to show us a perfect performance? How many late nights does a scientist spend in a lab before making that fateful discovery?

Hard work can seem daunting, but don't let it dampen the process of imagining your dream. Mary Lou Retton, the spunky gymnast who took home an Olympic gold medal in 1984 and has been interviewed hundreds of times since, is quick to point out that training never seemed like work to her.

She loved what she was doing. Being true to herself, even as a young girl, catapulted her to success. The same is true of the entrepreneur, who endured a number of "failures" by other people's judgment, before reaching the top.

Falling off the beam, losing another business, not getting the scientific result – these so-called "failures" are seen by active dreamers not as failures, but as *opportunities* to learn, grow and do it even better the next time. They turn what seems like weakness into strength.

"A goal without a plan is just a wish."
ANTOINE DESAINT-EXUPERY

Mapping Your Dream

These seven steps outline a sequence you can follow to manifest
your own vision. As you work through the exercises, keep these
steps in mind or review them occasionally to see where you are on
the road to your dreams.

- *Define your dream.* You need to know on what you are working
  or where you are moving toward. Set your sights on what you
  want and move toward it in the same way you would if you were
  planning a trip. Go from point A to point B to point C. Don't be
  limited by anything in your dreams.

- *Visualize what your dream would look like.* Who would be a part
  of it, where would you be? How long do you think it will take to
  get there?

- *Be aware of what is possible.* Find the truth behind your fantasy.
  You can always change things around if you need to, but some of
  your dream must be based on facts and tangible elements.

- *Be courageous.* Just having a dream is not enough. You have to
  have the determination to move forward, the courage to believe
  in yourself and the bravado to get the things you need to help
  you. You have to have what it takes, the moxy to say: *"I'm going
  to do this no matter what."* If you need a support system, figure
  out who your support system is. If you need to take some classes
  to get there, take them. If you need to ask questions, then ask.
  But ask the right people. Don't be afraid to call people you might
  not know. I've called many authors about their work. Have the
  courage to take risks.

- *Step out of yourself.* Be willing to let go of yourself for a little while and give to someone else. You can develop an appreciation for other people and even an appreciation for yourself. Learn compassion – how to feel for another human being. Treat others as you would want someone to treat you. Being compassionate elevates your self-image. And that gives you courage. Courage is an important part of realizing a dream.

- *Accept yourself for who you are.* Everyone has value. Self-confidence comes when you experience success. All you need is the smallest modicum of success to give you courage to take the next step.

- *Believe that it is never too late to realize your dreams.* You may have years behind you, but that does not mean there are not plenty ahead of you, too. A friend of mine wanted to get a doctorate in psychology. At the age of 36 she thought she was too old. "In four years I'll be forty," she lamented. My reply was, "In four years you'll be forty anyway. Why not be a Ph.D., too?"

"Dreams are today's answers to tomorrow's questions."
EDGAR CAYCE

JOURNALING IN PRACTICE

Meredith worked as a secretary for a large non-profit arts organization. She was a single mother, and at 35, led a busy and productive life. Although she liked her co-workers and the pace of her job, and enjoyed being a parent, she struggled to earn enough money and spend as much time with her children as she wanted.

She came to me because she felt that she needed to make some changes in her life, but she didn't know exactly what those changes could be. To explore what kind of change was ahead for Meredith, I asked her to begin a journal that focused on fantasy – a playful list of questions where she could unearth what was rumbling inside her.

Meredith wrote long passages about vacations in Italy, taking walks in fabulous gardens with her children and visiting museums. She fantasized about sitting in an overstuffed armchair, reading books for hours. Her journals were long, descriptive passages, artful in their own right, lush with detail. Meredith's journal writing focused on the aesthetic and personal. The artfulness of everyday life captivated her interest.

Over the course of weeks, I asked Meredith to imagine how she could attain this vision. As we soon learned, all along Meredith had been describing many aspects of her boss's life. She was an art historian and curator. Meredith was her administrator. She made her boss's travel plans, booked her lectures, contacted the museums and galleries before visits, and gathered research materials almost everyday. She knew lots of details about how her boss lived.

When we talked about her fantasy, Meredith revealed that she had never considered becoming an art historian before. She had studied art in college, but getting married, having children and now supporting them were in focus. Getting a Ph.D. at 35 seemed to her such a lofty goal. The years of school and training were daunting. But once the vision was created, the seed began to germinate.

She realized she had the best of resources: a boss who could answer many of her questions, arts resources at her fingertips each day at work, and first-hand knowledge of what her life could be. The road ahead would be long, but as Meredith learned, it would be just as long if she didn't pursue her dream.

*"Go confidently in the direction of your dreams.
Live the life you have imagined."*
HENRY DAVID THOREAU

QUESTIONS & EXERCISES I

FANTASIES

What do you fantasize about? What dreams are at the center of your core, at the base of your naked self? Can you identify what your spirit desires? To have a fantasy, you have got to have imagination, so you can "see" or "create" the world you want to live in. Can you visualize the scenario down to its smallest details? Can you see it vividly?

A dream or fantasy is something that you might be able to attain if the circumstances in your life were just a little different.

Think about it for a while, and then write down five or more fantasies you have had over a lifetime. Choose your three favorites.

_____

_____

_____

_____

_____

Why did you choose these three?

_____

_____

_____

_____

_____

Write down your most vivid fantasy.

_____

_____

_____

_____

_____

NOTES

QUESTIONS & EXERCISES II

STRONG DREAMS

What makes for a strong dream? The foundations are simple and logical. Build a base, a strong foundation for your dream by defining it and then building upon it, one brick at a time. Set a goal. It will give your dream a reality and a sense of urgency. Connect your dream with your strengths. How can your strengths enhance your dream? How can you use your strengths to move forward with your dream?

List your strengths (revisit Chapter 3) then list your dream.
Now, link your strengths and your dream. For example:

Strength	**Dream**
Perseverance, networking	Be a talent agent

Make your list and draw the links here:

NOTES

QUESTIONS & EXERCISES III

VISUALIZE

It is said that the most important element in manifesting a dream is in seeing it. The more vivid it is, the more details you can see, the more real it becomes. This process is known as "creative visualization." The following exercise is a way to visualize your dream.

Go through magazines and select pictures of everything that might create your fantasy world. Cut them out. Make a collage on this page, or on a larger sheet of paper. Choose all the images that feel good to you. Use words too, if you like. Whatever it takes to make your vision as real as possible.

Get used to seeing these images. They could be a summer home on the beach, a new coat, a new office or an image of yourself writing a script. Make it personal. Make it real. Use your imagination – and have fun!

NOTES

QUESTIONS & EXERCISES IV

FANTASY ISLAND
Where would you like to go today? The world is your oyster.
Find your pearl.

Where do you dream of going?

_____

_____

_____

_____

_____

What would it take to get there?

_____

_____

_____

_____

_____

**Find out the price, set a goal, time of year, who would you
go with.**

_____

_____

_____

_____

_____

NOTES

QUESTIONS & EXERCISES V

TURNING YOUR DREAM INTO REALITY
You might begin with this exercise: list everything you dream about doing in the next year, including promotions, relationships, purchases (car, home, apartment, etc.) and trips. Put a realistic time frame above each goal. For example: I'd really love to go to Hawaii for Christmas vacation.

_____

_____

_____

_____

_____

What would it take to be (do) that? List each dream. Next to it, list the steps you need to take to realize that dream.

_____

_____

_____

_____

What books can you read that might be helpful to you?

_____

_____

_____

_____

_____

What people do you need to meet to help you?

_____

_____

_____

_____

_____

Who can get you there faster? List these people and how you can reach them. List the time frame for contacting each person. Stay within your time frame.

_____

_____

_____

_____

_____

What else can be helpful to you and how do you plan to go about it?

_____

_____

_____

_____

_____

NOTES

"The future belongs to those
who believe in the beauty of their dreams."
ELEANOR ROOSEVELT

WEEK EIGHT

YOUR DREAM BECOMES REAL

Your dream can be as incredible as your imagination is creative.
Bringing it to your daily life requires yet another set of tools –
faith, commitment and step-by-step, concrete goals.

In this section, you will take your vision, whatever that vision may
be, into the practical world you already know. You will also learn to
work through smaller goals as building blocks to larger successes.

Believing

You can manifest anything you truly believe. But how do you
believe in something so far away? The key is to believe that your
dream is alive this very second. By connecting this moment to your
future, you are sketching an outline for what is ahead.

Imagine yourself achieving your goal, realizing your dream. Use
the creative visualization technique from your previous work. If
your dream is to own a house, imagine that house, take a walk
through its rooms, look outside its windows to what is there. Go
ahead, decorate the living room. Fill it with your favorite things.
Imagine friends coming over for dinner, enjoying the warmth and
company in the place of your dream.

Maybe you want to be a doctor. Imagine yourself now in a white coat, stethoscope hanging around your neck, smiling as your next patient walks through the door.

You are no longer waiting patiently for your dream to come true. It *is* coming true. In the next journal exercises, you will add more "evidence" – written evidence – that reinforces your belief. Affirm your dream everyday. When you first wake up in the morning, your first thought will be: "My dream *is* happening. I *am* successful." And it is true. Your dream is alive. Success is here and now.

Believing in your dream gives you guidance and belief in your short-term goals. It gives your short-term commitments resonance and meaning.

Tools for Commitment

Does it ever seem that when you make a commitment you have to run an obstacle course of unforeseen problems in order to keep the commitment? Do you think you just don't have enough willpower to make things happen? There is no one who has not struggled with what we call "willpower."

Willpower is a funny thing. We tell ourselves, "I will not eat dessert." "I will set aside money every week." "I will go to the gym three times a week." I will, I will, I will.

Famous last words. Why is it so hard to will ourselves to do what we know is in our own best interest, even when the goal is something small and absolutely attainable?

Here is the secret. "I will not eat dessert." Why? Why should you not eat dessert? Dessert is great! The reason you tell yourself this is because it will break your promise to lose or maintain weight. But telling yourself the words, "I need to lose weight" can hardly compete with the yummy piece of cake in front of you.

The problem is that the end goal, to lose or maintain weight, has been disconnected from the moment. You tell yourself it's only a piece of cake. "Just this once," you say. How do you break this cycle of thinking so that you are reconnected to your earlier point of resolve?

If your goal is to lose ten pounds before summer, you have to *imagine the end result*. You have to see yourself ten pounds lighter, wearing that favorite outfit. When you wake up in the morning, you picture it in your mind, you *positively reinforce* the image. Throughout the day, long before the cake is on a plate in front of you, you remind yourself of the image, or look at what you have written about this goal in your journal.

The *image* in your mind, even when the cake is offered, is a far more powerful tool than telling yourself you shouldn't, that you need to lose weight.

Saving money for a purpose, a greater purpose like buying a house, is much easier than saving money simply for the sake of saving. If you make a commitment to the house, the very one you toured in your imagination, then you will need far less "willpower" to avoid overspending on clothes or items you think are less important.

Another useful tool for keeping your shorter goal commitments is to measure your *performance goals* rather than outcomes. This should not be confused with setting *end* goals, or long-term objectives to pull you forward, but as a way to reward yourself and avoid the typical frustrations from missing a specific goal mark.

If your goal was to recover from a major muscle injury that was preventing you from walking, your end goal may be to walk again. Your *performance* goals would include learning ways to improve your exercise regime or time performing exercises.

Indeed, these are less complicated scenarios in the realization of your dream, but they represent how the small steps in everyday life are part of the building process. Commitment is much easier once your goals and dream are alive, imagined as real and connected to the present.

So don't be afraid to make a commitment to your goals, your
end goals. The goal you imagine will become like a magnet pulling
you forward, and the "willpower" to achieve it will be ready
and waiting.

Breaking It Down

In her book *Bird by Bird,* Anne LaMott tells the story of her
nine-year-old brother who was sitting at the dining room table
surrounded by stacks of research books about birds and a pad
of blank paper. He was crying uncontrollably.

When their father asked the boy what was wrong, he said he had
a report due on birds and he just couldn't do it. The father saw the
problem immediately. The task was too daunting, there were too
many books, and the boy was simply overwhelmed. "It's easy," he
said to his son. "Just take it *bird by bird.*"

Goals and dreams may be one and the same, but very often, setting
interim goals are part of a larger dream. You have likely heard of
short-term or long-term goals. One is more immediate, the other in
the distant future. When those goals are connected, they both take
on more meaning and substance. They give power to one another.
Your goals are yours alone. Keep in mind that imagining them
coming to life is a powerful tool for making them happen.

The questions at the end of this chapter encompass three types of
goals: personal, professional and spiritual. Personal goals are those
you have for yourself and your personal relationships.

Professional goals encompass the work place, your job or your
school. Perhaps you want to change careers mid-stream, move up
in your current one, or change your course of study.

Spiritual goals are those related to self-understanding. These goals
may coincide with a particular religion or philosophy, or they
may be based on values you prize from your observations in life.

Each of these scenarios has its own stepping path, so you need to use your imagination to look for that path. For instance, if you work in management and want to advance and earn more money, talk to others who have done the same. This also applies to major career changes.

Finding mentors for these transitions is one of the best ways to make large leaps in your professional life. If you know someone who works in a profession you would like to be in, find out how he or she can help. Even if you only know a person by reputation, be bold and contact him or her directly.

Here is an important bit of advice. Just as you would tell a friend who received a bad report from a doctor to get a second opinion, if you get news that discourages you from following the path to your goal, go for a second opinion.

Your support network should be just that, support. If you do not have others right now to support you, just go for it without any opinion other than your own singular belief.

*"The biggest adventure you can take
is to live the life of your dreams."*
OPRAH WINFREY

QUESTIONS & EXERCISES I

GENERAL GOALS

There are goals that are not attached to a higher purpose, but are
things you want to accomplish nevertheless. What are those goals?
Is it to have a general sense of well being? Is it healthier food?
Is it a personality issue, such as being too impulsive or impatient?
Is it buying a house? Publishing a book? Losing weight?
Think about what your overall goals are.

**List your short-term goals. What goals would you like to
achieve in the next six to twelve months?**

_____

_____

_____

_____

_____

**What are your long-term goals? What goals would you like to
achieve in the next one to five years?**

_____

_____

_____

_____

_____

NOTES

QUESTIONS & EXERCISES II

YOUR CAREER

Your career is an integral part of you. It takes up most of your days and consumes a lion's share of your life. Is your career your life's purpose or merely a job? Does it give you daily satisfaction? What does your career mean to you? Are you doing what you love to do?

List some of your professional goals:

_____

_____

_____

_____

_____

Where do you want to go in your career?

_____

_____

_____

_____

_____

Do you feel that a different job is within your reach? If so, what would it take for you to get it? For example: Do you need to rewrite your resume, focusing on different skills? Do you need to change the way you dress?

_____

_____

_____

_____

_____

What type of work would you do if you could choose your career path? Be realistic.

_____

_____

_____

_____

_____

Are you passionate about your work? If so, what do you like about what you do? If not, what would you change?

_____

_____

_____

_____

_____

What are your talents? List them.

_____

_____

_____

_____

_____

How do you use your talents to achieve your professional goals?

_____

_____

_____

_____

_____

Is your job interwoven with your life's purpose? Clarify once again in writing what you think your life's purpose is. Stop, think, relax. Close your eyes and ask yourself this question. Answer the best way you can.

_____

_____

_____

_____

_____

NOTES

QUESTIONS & EXERCISES III

PERSONAL, FAMILY, RELATIONSHIP GOALS

Our dreams don't stand alone. They rest within us, within the world we live in and within the people with whom we live. Do you dream of having a better relationship with those who are in your life? Do you wish to find a loving relationship with the partner of your dreams? How do your dreams fit within your world?

How do you feel about the life and the world that you have created for yourself?

_____

_____

_____

_____

What about your friends? Why do you encircle yourself with them?

_____

_____

_____

_____

What kind of relationships do you want to have in your life?

_____

_____

_____

_____

How do you plan on achieving these goals and attracting these people?

_____

_____

_____

_____

_____

NOTES

QUESTIONS & EXERCISES IV

PRIORITIZING YOUR GOALS

Break the circle into pie shaped wedges that represent the way you allocate your time to your current goals: emotional, personal, familial, professional, leisure time.

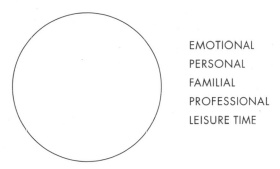

EMOTIONAL
PERSONAL
FAMILIAL
PROFESSIONAL
LEISURE TIME

Take a good look at what you have drawn. Do you want to rearrange anything? How would you like to change it? That is, how much time would be ideal for each aspect of your life?

In this circle, how would your time be allocated if you changed your priorities?

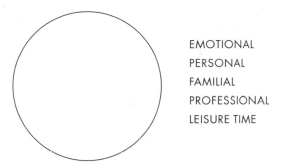

EMOTIONAL
PERSONAL
FAMILIAL
PROFESSIONAL
LEISURE TIME

NOTES

QUESTIONS & EXERCISES V

ACCOMPLISHING GOALS

The difference between a pipe dream and realizing a goal is action. You must actively make your dreams come true. It may not be easy at times, but with determination, you can and will achieve what you have set out to do. Go back to Questions & Exercises I of this section and examine your short-term goals.

NOTES

"Every blade of grass has its Angel that bends over it
and whispers, 'Grow, grow.'"
The Talmud

CHAPTER 5

FINDING YOUR SOUL

Your soul is at the core of your naked self. It is the essence of who
you are and what you are becoming. But it is often difficult for us
to perceive that we have a soul. Here is a story that illustrates this
dilemma of modern life:

Once upon a time there was a man who lived in a small town.
One night he fell asleep and dreamt that God spoke to him. In his
dream, the man heard God warning him of an impending flood that
would wash away the entire town. Then the man heard God tell
him not to worry because God would save him.

The next day, it began to rain. It rained and it rained. The water
rose quickly, and the man climbed out of a second-floor window
and sat on his roof. He sat and he prayed and he watched as the
floodwater continued rising to the level of the roof. Soon the police
came in a small boat and urged him to climb onto the boat. He
refused, saying that God would rescue him. He continued praying,
firm in his belief that he would be saved by God.

A couple of hours later, the water had risen so high that the roof
was almost covered. Another larger boat arrived, and a group of
people on the boat begged the man to leap from the roof and swim
to the boat. Again he refused, saying God would save him.

By now the sun was beginning to set, but the water kept rising. Soon the water was up to the man's nose. He kept praying, certain in his belief that God would save him.

Suddenly, a helicopter appeared overhead and extended a ladder down to the man. The pilot and the crew beckoned him to grab hold of the ladder, but again the man refused, saying "God will care for me. My faith is with him." So the helicopter left.

Soon the water swept the man off the roof and he drowned. When he arrived in heaven, he said to God, "You appeared to me in my dream and you promised you would save me. I prayed and prayed to you, but you didn't save me!" And God replied: "First, I sent the police in a little boat and you sent them away. Next I sent a larger boat, and you dismissed that. Finally I sent you a helicopter! What more did you want?"

Here's the moral of the story: Every thing you need to save yourself is right there in front of you. But you have to see what's in front of you.

It takes three elements combined to make a whole person – the mind, the body and the soul. We've addressed issues of mind and body, now it's time to complete the whole person with special attention to the soul.

The soul is the unspoken piece that is so often missing in analysis. Many therapists do not recognize its importance. It is as if they say, "Leave your body and soul outside and just bring me your mind and voice."

Some people are afraid to discuss the soul. Perhaps that is because the soul defies easy explanation and because discussions about the soul often take on a religious dimension. But you don't have to be religious to believe that your soul is a very important part of who you are and how you deal with life.

Although the soul transcends the *here and now*, it also puts you right smack in the middle of the *here and now*. When you're in touch with your soul, you can appreciate life. You appreciate the flowers and the sun. You appreciate the Universe.

Our soul creates the uniqueness of *who* we are. When you find your soul within yourself, you unleash the potential to be all that you can be. It is the connection to the soul that provides boundless levels of awareness. If you open your heart and mind, your soul can awaken your spirit and you can find out what the true purpose of your life is. It is a leap of faith in the universal belief that we are not alone.

"The soul of man is a lamp of God
searching all the chambers of the womb."
Proverbs 20:20

Recognizing Your Inner Life

The soul is often equated with light. When a person reaches another realm of understanding he often says, "I see the light." We hear the phrase and automatically understand him. But what does he actually mean by this? A *light*ness of being, of spirit? He feels *light*hearted. His eyes are filled with lightness. This person is enlightened by his soul.

The light radiates from a world beyond our bodies. It is the essence of God, if you believe in God, the essence of a world that is bigger than yours. It is the universal connection between man and God, which is why words cannot begin to articulate the power of its source.

The soul is called light because it is a small spark of divine essence. It is about believing in ourselves and taking a leap of faith that there is a world beyond us that can help and support us.

The soul creates a zone of calm, a balance between mind, body and spirit. With this wisdom, you can begin to distinguish between what is good for you, (as in "healthy") and what is damaging for you. Your body houses your soul. When your soul feels treaded upon, your body feels lost. Hence the expression, "a lost soul."

When you meet someone who seems to touch the very core of your being, you might say "he's touched my soul." When you meet someone and have a soul-to-soul connection, you might say "I've met my soul mate."

Again, this section is about understanding that deep within you exists the potential to go one step beyond where you are. It is about having faith in yourself and faith in the Universe. The Universe is a major resource of information. The Universe provides. Ask a question and the Universe will answer. But you have to know when your helicopter has arrived.

You can connect to your soul. But first you must believe you *have* a soul. Ask yourself, "Do I believe that I have a soul?" Then ask, "Am I in touch with my soul?"

These are important questions. People gravitate toward people with soul. If you pay close attention, the people you do not like are usually people who are not in touch with their souls. They are closed off. Think about it: Who are the people in your life you would call *soulful* people? What is it that makes them soulful to you?

Honesty, integrity, genuineness, compassion are strong elements of the soul, particularly compassion. Compassion is feeling for another person and wanting to extend your self toward him or her. Remember the saying: Don't judge your friend until you have lived in his place?

In extending yourself towards another human being, the goal is not to do it so you can look good but to actually connect to the other person. Having compassion makes that intimate connection. It says *I understand how you feel.* If you do this only because you think it is the right thing to do, that's more mechanical. If you do it because you really do feel compassion, now you are touching on the precipice of your soul.

"Nothing can cure the soul but the senses,
just as nothing can cure the senses but the soul."
OSCAR WILDE, *The Picture of Dorian Gray, 1891*

WEEK NINE

LIGHT WITHIN THE DARKNESS
I've designed six-days of exercises, which, I hope, will help you connect with your soul. Don't expect perfection on the first try, however. It's not as easy as it appears.

DAY 1: Kindness
The indelible power of kindness leaves a mark on all those it touches. Have you ever forgotten a kind act? Eric Hoffer once said, *"Kindness is its own motive. We are made kind by being kind."* When you are feeling sad or blue, a kind act is the remedy for your soul.

Do a random act of kindness. Sometimes you want credit for your kindness. We all want to be validated and recognized. This assignment is the highest act of kindness, the anonymous kind. You give for the sake of giving.

Notes on Day 1: Do a random act of kindness. What did you do? Who was it for? At the end of the day, how did you feel?

_____

_____

_____

_____

_____

"I want friends, not admirers. People who respect me
for my character and my deeds, not my flattering smile.
The circle around me would become much smaller,
but what does that matter, as long as they're sincere?"
ANNE FRANK, *March 7, 1944*

DAY 2: Deeds

George Eliot once said, "*Our deeds determine us as much as we
determine our deeds.*" The deeds we perform are who we become.
Our deeds are what define us, shape us, and connect us to our
community and our soul.

Do a good deed that brings you closer to the world. Now buy
something that connects you to nature. It can be a flower, a plant,
candle (connect by watching the light of the flames).

**Notes on Day 2: What is a deed? It is an act, as opposed to
words. (*Actions speak louder than words.*) Describe how you
felt after doing your good deed today.**

DAY 3: Altruism

What is altruism? Altruism is the selfless regard for the well being of
others. It is the ultimate generosity of the soul. And, this selfless regard
for our fellow beings, the ability to tap into complete compassion and
act on it has been an earmark of enlightened beings.

Pick a charity and volunteer to help for just one evening. Helping others
will make you feel good about yourself. (And you may want to keep
doing it in the future.)

Notes on Day 3: Do you feel differently after you have volunteered? Describe that feeling.

_____

_____

_____

_____

_____

DAY 4: Gratitude

With gratefulness, the world shines brighter, for we appreciate every action and every morsel of life. Gratitude opens doors of communication and draws people to you. Being thankful brings respect for life and encourages positive actions. It is our first steps toward peace and grace.

Write a thank-you prayer to whichever God or higher power you believe in. Write specific examples of all the gifts you have in your life. Write it on an index card. This becomes your "prayer" that you can carry with you wherever you go.

Copy your prayer here:

_____

_____

_____

_____

_____

DAY 5: Taking Care of Yourself

All of us need to take care of ourselves. It's important to treat yourself with respect and goodness. It gives you a time to relax and connect with your soul without the distractions of your daily routine. Be uncommonly kind to yourself. Don't expect perfection at the first try and don't think it's easy. It's not.

**Notes on Day 5: What will you give yourself today?
For example: I will give myself an hour without my cell phone.
I will listen to music without interruption for an hour. I will take myself to a yoga class.**

_____

_____

_____

_____

_____

DAY 6: Positive Attitude

Gandhi said, _"Resentment is taking poison and expecting the other person to die."_ Try not to criticize. Spend this day trying to let go of the anger and resentment that you may have towards another person. Be aware of the power of speech and try not to criticize anyone for an entire day, including yourself.

Notes on Day 6: How did you stop yourself from thinking negative thoughts about people in your life?

_____

_____

_____

_____

_____

> "The roots of true achievement
> lie in the will to become the best
> that you can become."
> HAROLD TAYLOR

CLOSURE

Congratulations! You have achieved a truly marvelous task.

Through the process of the last nine weeks, you have become acquainted with your naked self, begun a dialogue with your inner guidance and refined a powerful relationship – your relationship to yourself. You will never be alone in a situation or with a decision. You have the ability to call upon the higher power that is within you. Use that power wisely and with the full force of your creative energy.

Always follow your dreams and pursue your purpose in life with full command. Trust your spirit – it will always guide you.

Good luck, good health and best wishes to you as you continue on your journey.

✂ ┄┄

GUIDEPOSTS
1. Sometimes bad things really do happen to good people. Don't let it stop you from being the best that you can be.
2. You cannot make anyone love you.
3. When you do find love, love with all your heart and soul.
4. Don't be afraid to feel vulnerable. It's the key to allowing love to happen.
5. Sometimes you have to be with someone through all the seasons before you can say "I love you."
6. Evil does exist, but it doesn't mean you have to make it your dating partner.
7. Progress is good, as long as it doesn't get in the way of your life. *(Continued on back)*

8. Just when you feel that you can't hold on anymore, remember that the sun is just around the corner, waiting to shine its glorious rays on you.
9. Be careful what you say – the Universe is listening.
10. Your body remembers what your mind chooses to forget.
11. Only you can bring meaning to your life.
12. There are always consequences to lies.
13. Be open to the suffering of others. Have compassion, even if you can't relieve someone else's suffering.
14. Be responsible for everything you do, but realize that you are not responsible for others' mistakes.
15. Be prepared. Do your homework – in school, at work, and above all, in life.

ABOUT THE AUTHOR

Janis Altman is an expert on building healthy relationships. In her role as advocate, speaker, trainer and healer, Janis draws strength from a range of experiences. She has spent more than 25 years empowering people to deal successfully with complex family and relationship issues.

As a practicing psychotherapist and life coach, Janis has delivered keynote presentations at Harvard, Columbia, Barnard, New York University, Cornell and other major universities. She has run seminars and workshops for American Express, Philip Morris, Disney and other Fortune 500 companies and has spoken or lectured at every major hospital in the New York metropolitan area.

While a staff consultant at Cornell University, her expert advice was showcased in magazines such as *Tango, Life and Style, Us Weekly* and *Newsweek*. In 1999, Janis was featured as an online Relationship/Advice Columnist on Disney Corporation's renowned *Family.com* website.

She is former Director of Training at New York City's Victim Services Agency (now Safe Horizons). While there, Janis led workshops for top municipal officials on a variety of critical intervention and prevention topics. She also co-founded and was Executive Director of the Institute for Growth and Development.

Janis has won respect as an expert in self-esteem and relationship training, family violence, crisis intervention, work-life balance and dance therapy and is a recognized leader in the emerging field of positive preventative therapy.

Currently she spends time seeing clients, running individual private workshops at schools and institutions and is teaching a course at Touro College on dance/movement therapy. She also lectures extensively in high schools throughout the Northeast and is in the process of completing two other books.

Janis is a cum laude graduate of Queens College, and has a master's degree in psychology and dance therapy from New York University.